CORIOLANUS IN DEUTSCHLAND

STEVEN BERKOFF is well known as an actor, playwright and theatre director. His work for the stage includes: *East*, which won critical acclaim for its originality and eclectic concoction of Elizabethan verse and punk poetry with Cockney slang, and its sequel *West*, which tells the story of Beowulf; *Greek*, which is a modern version of the Oedipus myth; and *Decadence, Harry's Christmas, Kvetch, Acapulco, Sink the Belgrano,* and *Massage.*

He has also rewritten *Agamemnon* (after Aeschylus) and *The Fall of the House of Usher* (from Edgar Allan Poe) and has dramatised three of Kafka's works — *The Trial, Metamorphosis* and *In the Penal Colony.*

A photographic study of his work, *The Theatre of Steven Berkoff*, was published in 1992 and he is currently in the process of writing his autobiography.

STEVEN BERKOFF

Coriolanus
in Deutschland

AMBER LANE PRESS

Published in 1992 by
Amber Lane Press Ltd
Cheorl House, Church Street,
Charlbury, Oxford OX7 3PR
Telephone 0608 810024

Printed and bound in Great Britain by
Dotesios Ltd, Trowbridge, Wiltshire

ISBN 1 872868 08 8

Introduction

From time to time I have gravitated to Germany to direct plays and first experienced the German theatre when Günther Beelitz, who was then the theatre administrator in Düsseldorf, asked me to direct my adaptation of Kafka's *The Trial*. It was in 1976 and I recall the intensity of that experience so well and to be in Germany *is* an intense experience. Everything seems to taste stronger, feel keener, the winters colder, the summers hotter, the language fiercer and more expressive, and the Düsseldorf Schauspielhaus itself was a hothouse of activity that embraced, under Beelitz's administration, a wide variety of styles, since he would trawl the world looking for directors to give his theatre the cultural mix he sought.

In Germany, with few exceptions, the Intendant, or administrator, is the artistic director who doesn't direct, in much the same way as our opera administrators, and consequently is free to travel and research other talents from many lands. Hence I was offered work in Europe before I was ever approached here in England.

I gained a reputation in Düsseldorf with *The Trial*, which won instant approval from the press and the public, and which had the flavour of German, which was, of course, its natural home. Like Joseph K, I had a small apartment and my breakfast came on the dot of 8 o'clock each day and the eggs and rolls were no less than perfect, washed down with that lovely German coffee.

So I waited some years before repeating that experience and in that time I had directed my first Shakespeare outside England, for another company, in New York, and for another marvellous administrator, the late Joe Papp. He had seen my work over the years and rang me one morning to ask me to direct *Coriolanus*, which I did, and somehow miraculously it turned out well, which goes to show that there is a solution to everything. So when I bumped into Günther in London at the stage door of the Queen's Theatre, where we had both seen *The Cherry Orchard*, directed by Robert Sturua, our conversation turned to work and he liked the idea of my directing *Coriolanus* in German. This time it would be in Munich, where I had never directed before but knew it only from a trip there years earlier performing *The Fall of the House of Usher* in a small fringe theatre. So I went to Munich and the following is a journal I kept at the time.

A journal is a very personal thing if you wish it to be or it can be objective and self-censoring; basically it should allow you to discharge your radioactive bile deep into the pages of your journal never to be seen and thus relieve you of the need to verbally annoy, castigate or scream. It is a friend that also filters out your thoughts and develops a line of reasoning. It is a companion and plaything and a way of doodling with words and even coming to some form of solution. It is not wise to censor too much and I found myself sometimes having to expunge certain thoughts since they were inflamed by the heat of the moment and read in cold blood later might appear unduly caustic. However, having said that, there were times when I had to state what happened in bold language to record what I felt was sometimes a conflict of values and ideology. There was, I felt, too much a desire to order things to a pre-arranged scheme of this is how we do things and even if the play was going well there was an attempt to deny its virtues because the methodology was different. My method was more casual but the effects were just as vital, as would be seen at the end.

From the beginning there seemed to be a recipe for trouble since there was not an element that seemed to be right. At first the translation, then the director who didn't sit down and 'talk' to them all at length, since I prefer to work it out on the floor, then the time factor, and so on . . . However, the actors did eventually come round and eventually we produced what I thought was a first-class show and even superior to the New York production, and I was very proud of it, and I am grateful to all the actors for sticking to it, to Günther for asking me to do it, and to Sona who helped me keep sane with her enthusiasm which made itself felt in her constant expressions of support. How one needs this at times. So in the final analysis we came through. This journal is an investigation of some of the torments I had with the company, with the play and with Munich, but I forgive them as I hope they will me.

Steven Berkoff
London, 1992

Thursday 18th April

Plane to Munich to do workshops for my forthcoming production of *Coriolanus* — big joke . . . The pilot announces that we are flying over Dachau! Stupid comment, when he could say that he is going over Munich. Dachau is famous for one thing — *a death camp!* — and we are flying Lufthansa.

The Trial at the National Theatre is working out and I will play Titorelli 44 times. At the same time I will be preparing *Kvetch*.

Munich, the theatre. A sense of oppressive heat in the foyer but the bars are laid out with utter perfection, neat ordered sandwiches, beautifully filled and cut, glasses artistically arranged, orange juice in mini-clusters. The ushers sit reading newspapers while waiting for the interval. Feeling of hopelessness and death . . . The area outside the theatre is litterless and not a single scrap of paper mars its orderliness as cars make their steady 30 miles per hour way along the darkened street. A couple of cycles pedal away. Nothing out of the way. Nothing in disarray. In the foyer the tables are neatly set out. The immaculate bar staff creatively arrange the precious sandwiches like we are in a five-star hotel.

The Prince Regent Theatre was built in the latter part of the nineteenth century and was designed to house Wagner's operas. It is utterly beautiful in a mock rococo, with pillared walls and gilded capitals and authentic wooden seats. A giant box is situated at the back of the theatre for VIPs and I can imagine Hitler sitting there, having a good time, since I am informed he lived only around the corner in a large house facing the park.

The prompter sits in the front row centre with the book! She rests one of her legs on a stool. She wears black with a white collar. I look up, as you do in a theatre when you are confined and all you can move is your neck upwards. I make this trajectory with my head, taking in the ornate ceiling with its ornamental floral motif. The audience is mostly middle- to old-aged, with a couple of young people dotted here and there. A young woman next to me works down the hem of her very mini skirt now that a male sits next to her. Her black stockings have a large diamond pattern and they remind me of other parts of the body.

The prompter gets her hand ready to open the prompt book. She wears her hair in a ballerina style and has an aquiline nose — probably a retired dancer seeking to be 'near' the theatre. Lights out. The prompter flings the book open. Swinish characters shouting a lot. Actors with funny voices. A woman enters wearing a tight satin dress . . . The king reminds me of Hilton Edwards, who was a large Irish queen and actor-manager of the Gate Theatre, Dublin. This actor, fit and crop-haired, seems to be over-relishing the part that fiction bestows on the unfamous. Lots of tableaux to canned music. An eccentric 'Englishman' stuttering German with an English accent . . . Every cliché imaginable, cold, heartless. My lack of language enables me to feel the cold blast of their emotion without the comforting tunic of comprehension, which helps you to filter it through your own memory zone. Naturally, a midget runs around.

A bed scene: girls with fig leaves sewn on to their crotches stand around in flesh-coloured tights pretending to be naked. They make half-hearted attempts to masturbate but perform as if they were ashamed of what they are being forced to do. A fat grizzled man comes on in a sedan, which then falls apart. Many man-hours must have gone into building this effect, which lasts about a minute. Then a young man with a distinctly hooked nose, making curious shapes with his mouth while speaking very loud, plays with a young woman in tights and leaps on to the bed. Everything seems heartless, whiny, mechanical, like a bad Feydeau farce.

I study my watch — the girl next to me pulls down her skirt once more. I notice that apart from the diamond pattern on her stockings there is a regular line of black dots.

The prompter keeps a moving finger on the page. The curtains tantalise me by drawing several times but then open again for a quick change. The 'Englishman' has a limp while another kicks his legs mechanically. I imagine that the director has asked his creative cast to find some foible, a characteristic. A blonde voluptuous piece comes on and twirls a gun like Calamity Jane and then pouts and grins for the rest of the evening. Another lady appears in body stocking and white tights which come halfway to her thighs and, from there down, pale white stockings. My eyes are glued to her crotch. I don't know why, but her extra-long white legs seem to be avenues of flesh leading to her pelvis and the gusset. The actors are getting on my nerves and suddenly I despise my profession. I see through the little tricks, the thrill of being before a trapped audience, the sidelong glances they direct to them, the pretence of listening with absorption. I imagine the chat offstage . . . the usual "It went well tonight," or "Funny audience, weren't they?" when through laziness or indifference they didn't get their usual quota of laughs . . . Suddenly wonder what the hell I am doing here. The curtain descends mercifully, thus blotting out another pointless evening in the Prince Regent Theatre, Munich.

The audience clap politely, not too much enthusiasm, but at least another payment to the god of guilt and we made ourselves absorb some culture. The actors come on one at a time . . . for some there is even a little bravoing and for others a modest clap. The girls are very attractive and are used mostly for humiliating life-wasting poses. I sense their abjection covering the hope that this will lead to better things. The audience shuffle out and an army of cloakroom attendants deliver their coats . . . a lot of them light cigarettes . . .

My driver takes me to a dreary hotel, a really low-grade kind of traveller's lodge that Gregor Samsa might have stayed at before he became a beetle. I look at the room . . . a tiny single bed like a grave. I pick up my bags and clear out, call a cab, which takes me to another hotel, the four-star Bayerische. A porter carries my luggage . . . there is a Keller downstairs . . . at least I feel better. Some delicious German Frankenwein is soon cascading down my throat . . . better still, frankfurters and sauerkraut . . . I feel myself again.

Friday 19th April

This morning after breakfast I was invited to view some more execrable garbage in one of the small studio theatres. It was a dress rehearsal of some modern play and there was a lot of shouting and screaming. Then, the whole point of my visit: The Workshop. Did one hour and three quarters of voice and mime. Sweated my guts out and wasn't really dressed for it but was able to entertain for the duration.

Herr Beelitz, the Director, refuses to pay the difference for the hotel, which I find unimaginably cheap of him and corrodes my desire to direct Coriolanus. It must be some kind of strange obsession with the law, since he is always quoting that it's 'against the rules' to pay more than 80 Marks (about £25) for the room and that other directors stay there. This was not borne out, in fact, when later on I stayed at a very comfortable small hotel. However, it seems mighty insulting to put a director of a major company in such a depressing hole . . . curious people, these Germans.

This hotel business convinces me that I do not wish to escape any more. Do *Coriolanus* in the UK, not here. Want to get out of this cold-blooded bastard country . . .

I hate the idea of the second Workshop tomorrow but leaving now will appear cowardly, and yet I can't stand any more, the loneliness and isolation and sitting eating alone again. I could go in tomorrow to complete my side of the bargain but since I no longer wish to spend six weeks in Germany directing *Coriolanus* the bravest thing would be to leave. I don't want to bring this Lessing play to London, as Günther has suggested, and I don't want to do *Coriolanus* and I don't want to do another Workshop, so why do it? Maybe to prove that I can. *The Trial* looms up and suddenly I don't want to do this either. I've got a vocal bug, or rather I have a bug about creating choral vocal effects with the company. I did it easily enough years ago but now I feel it to be an imposition on the team to stand in front of them and create sounds. If it comes naturally and freely I will do it and I remember when I did *The Trial* in Düsseldorf how easily we created the vocal effects, which were one of the high points of the show, the choral sound and music underpinning and creating atmosphere. Now we will have the great voice teacher, Patsy Rodenberg.

I'm back in the Keller of my hotel and I like it. It's a place to go and eat at large wooden tables and drink good wine.

The whole place is gemütlich . . . and yet how different in temperament to LA and my joy there, compared with my misery here. Give me the guts to leave and reduce my pain. Even during the show tonight my pulse rate shot up, which proves that bad theatre is not good for your health, since you feel trapped and cannot escape. I went backstage to congratulate the actors and asked Karlheinz if he would have a drink with me since I didn't want another evening alone, but he had been invited to Günther's house to see photos of their South American tour. He seemed slightly abashed to realise that the director of the theatre had not invited his guest director. Turd! Just go!

Bad night but slept . . . not felt this torture for a long time, force-fed German hysteria, pseudo-German candidness, sexual depravity, ugliness and remoteness from all art forms. This desire to appear liberated and at the centre of the social problems of the world seems to obsess this theatre at the moment, as if the will was sick and the world was a sick world only. Plays about abortions and sexual harassment. Large photos in the foyer of this elegant theatre of women with skirts up and flying and it's all a little too "the lady doth protest too much". . . I should love to leave on the next flight and never see them again. A hideous ugliness manifests itself like a miasma around my head in this beautiful town which I have not explored. And I wish I could go. I feel bad since all the bastards will turn up and it is a special strength to stay, but don't work your guts out like yesterday. Make them work and get out straight away. This is *clean!* Otherwise there will be a slight taint. They all turn up and then are turned away. They can't reach everyone to cancel. This *feels* better now, even through the torture. At least the Germans can't blame the guilty Jew, but no show of his shall pollute my shores. *The Trial* jumps in my head again, which I must start next week and I try to think of the sound workshops I did in Düsseldorf. I sweat to think of it and my pulse races.

Saturday 20th April

Yet another play.

Much screaming . . . A woman stuffs Kleenex in her crotch but for what reason I am not quite sure. Another keeps smashing cakes and I try to imagine that these must represent foetuses, since the play deals with the problems of abortion. Günther tells me earnestly that abortion is not legal in Germany except for special cases and I must say that in the circumstances Germany would be against anything and everything that had to do with the shortening or terminating of life! He seems to feel that a worthy play needs to evaluate the issues. Unlike the grand main theatre, this is the 'studio', hence a display of 'graffiti' on the outside wall, skilfully done and obviously commissioned to show street cred where there is none. But it is good to be in touch with 'Yoof'.

We come to the end of the rehearsal, which was replete with singing angels and a trio of villainous men like a satanic chorus, much screaming and some bed scenes. All vaguely worthy in that phoney working-class theatre style that loves to be real. They really feel that by taking off trousers or tights, standing naked, genitals socially exposed like the liberation of the workers from their chains while the petit bourgeois audience have their left-wing consciences massaged before going out to dinner, they have made a statement for the under-privileged.

After the rehearsal the four dramaturgs (those who earn a living by amplifying the director's needs and making informative thick programmes with ample quotes) give notes and notes and notes. My friend Karlheinz tells me that this can go on for hours. Is he kidding me?

Night: a bright yellow stage.

Günther Beelitz has me seeing everything in order to find my cast and I have to sit through hour after hour of unmitigating stodge, although tonight's show was a well acted, though narcissistic, piece of East German bollocks. Much vitality, even in this shit, which was an updated and totally incoherent version of a Lessing play. The play, according to a German actor, had been lost in the treatment that it was given and so the show was a group of actors playing out its themes.   I found it loathsome and tricky and, although of East German origin, in keeping with the West German *drek*. The actresses indulged in their 'freedom' and posed and pouted and surrealed all over the place. A kind of "What can we do now with this prop?" A kind of free-wheeling free association. I don't want to stay but hang in to the end. The lead actor is very good and tremendously energetic. His name is Rufus Beck and he will be playing Coriolanus although I don't know this as yet. The women are beautiful in a way that few British actresses aspire to. I mean, here they are sexy and powerful. We like our actresses in Britain to be a little like a solid tweed coat, hard-wearing, well made, keeps you warm and is authentic, but you don't get turned on.

The keynote of the Lessing play is surrealism and the programme shows a Man Ray creation, the iron (domestic) with nails sticking out of its base . . . The two women in the play are leashed like tigresses. The male changes his clothes for a dress after coming on stage soaking wet, for what reason is not clear, like they have been swimming fully dressed. They make a mock modest show of undressing, trying to cover themselves while getting out of their wet things . . . Much fun is had . . . Reminds me of a Rowan Atkinson sketch when he undresses on the beach and puts his swimsuit on without taking off his trousers since he is bashful in front of a leering spectator. The actor continues and we are treated to a brief glimpse of his balls hanging down. Do I wish to see this? Does it matter? I am afraid to admit to a sneaking vein of prudery in me. But this is Germany and this is the Prince Regent Theatre.

The actress now peels off her knickers the way women do when it looks as if they are a second roll of skin. The actor simulates intercourse but then ends up frantically masturbating and in his frenzy the front row of the stalls is sprayed with his saliva . . . The woman breaks her string of pearls and of course he puts them in her mouth. The director has allowed the actors to follow their noses and of course this 'behaviourism' is a school of thought. In improvisation you can do anything that may trigger off the next thought which is born of it until the thoughts dwindle off. While in greater improvisers like Chaplin it is a free-roaming guide to his genius, here it is a kind of guide to the kindergarten. The school of surrealism mustn't flag and so now a box is brought in . . . A knife appears from within and cuts its way out . . . OK, that's not so awful since a woman appears like a birth from a cardboard womb . . . The woman tears off a piece of newspaper for the man to wipe the sperm off his hands and then throws the crumpled paper at the audience. How bold! An actor sitting next to me, who had been at my afternoon Workshop, bravely throws the paper back. Bravery? We the audience are treated like shit; there is something intimidating about being accosted from the stage. The actors appear to be having a good time while we squirm, but it's a time without soul, humour or spirit, it's a good time like the destruction of civilisation. Is this the post-Hitler revolt? Is this the other side of the coin? Does the pendulum have to drop the whole way down before balance is restored? The man has an impressive voice and screeches in admirable falsetto. A fat father now comes on worrying about his daughter, a young girl in a little nymphet's white dress who enters and starts screaming. I consult my watch at what seem to be 30-second intervals. This is a sick evening.

At least I am glad not to return to that cheapo hotel, although the nice secretary confirmed that the 'Law' does not allow them to pay more than 80 Marks for a hotel and Günther cheerfully repeated it. Running three theatres as he does he still seems to have time to be concerned about £25 for a hotel room. I admire his proficiency. The evening winds on. The young members of the audience seem to like it. After all, it's so different from the politeness of the clean streets and ordered homes and genteel coffee-houses. I stare at my watch. I must get out, but there is a row of people to negotiate. Now the very pretty actress crouches on her high heels, occasionally revealing a splash of her white knickers, accidentally as it were . . . I'm not complaining . . . The man reappears in a suit and both dance furiously, having started slow and, of course, taking it to its absurd limits. The style becomes predictable. The little girl now finds a tuba which she proceeds to blow irritatingly. The man now chases them round with a cardboard tube, the kind you wrap material around. He hits the floor with it and, of course, it breaks and, of course, he sticks his arm in the two halves so he looks like a freak with tubes for arms and, of course, he tries to walk with them as legs . . . of course . . . of course. IT ENDS! The cast come on beaming. They had a good time . . . They seem terribly pleased with their breakthrough in modern art. Thank God poor Lessing is dead: however, the actors did perform with a lot of energy. To what end it may be debated, but shadows crawled across my mind.

I return to my hotel debased and full of self-loathing. I sit in the Keller for the second night alone and contemplate my bratwurst then book my return flight a day earlier. I like Munich with its soft hotels with warm yellow glows from amber shades as the dark grey of evening draws in, and the Bierkeller with its shadows of drinking men. On the cold winter nights you can sit in coffee-houses and write and drink thick tomato soup with a dollop of cream in it.

Friday 31st May

Six weeks since my first investigative workshops in Munich and now, after doing Titorelli in *The Trial* at the National I am back for a week to do some preliminary rehearsals of *Coriolanus*. The benefit of doing repertoire is that you can fit in other work.

In the evening I am met at the airport by two of the theatre chappies; one is Dieter Opitz, who is Günther's assistant and a very charming, friendly man; the other is the dramaturg. They actually meet me with a small bottle of champagne, which I find very surprising. I don't want to go straight to the hotel and so we go instead to Leopoldstrasse and sit in an outdoor café where I have spaghetti and wine and have a really good night and am even happy. I am starting to communicate more with these people.

Saturday 1st June

Suddenly I am living in Munich near a gentle garden by the Hotel Prince Regent. A good breakfast. The density of German life around me, the stronger smells, the well-tiled overlapping design on the roofs, pine trees in the garden. Opposite my room in the building facing the hotel somebody has erected a little pigeon box. A pleasant sensation floods through me now as I could be here forever. In my room I attempt to open my window onto the terrace but fail to determine the secret until the cleaner shows me how it opens like a window and also like a door!

This is a perfect place to think and learn *Kvetch*. Before I left for Munich Nick Grace came over to read the part of Hal and looking at it again gave me a sense of how my range has stretched in recent years. Nick was very friendly and effusive when he came in, kissing me on the cheek and expressing unfeigned delight in the play. However, most of the value of the reading was to restore confidence in myself and my faith in the play. Günther tells me he likes going to Russia, Israel and East Germany. I expect he finds them more 'real' and it does allow him to be large and beneficent and even helps the poor theatre groups of those nations like Israel to visit Germany.

It's a sunny day over a well-ordered Munich and I walk to work and through the courtyard; the fountain sparkles in the morning sunlight. The doors are locked and I can't find my way in. Eventually I enter the main entrance where they are cleaning, and gaze at the charming and elegant theatre once more, with its mock boxes on the outer walls. It's really the opera house, the drama theatre is temporarily in residence until their building is repaired at the end of the year. I return to the courtyard and watch two ducks swimming in the tiny bowl that is filled by the fountain looking like they are toys in a bath. Eventually my dramaturg turns up and we enter the rehearsal room. I make an attempt to concentrate and sit behind a table where already there appears to be an army of people . . . one translator, naturally, one assistant, one dramaturg, another translator/assistant, one prompter and the assistant of the theatre. Some directors love their little army, their mini-audience, and are not happy unless there is a phalanx of bodies behind them; whereas I exude more freedom unshackled by a retinue taking down notes every time the director breaks wind, sharing out the responsibilities and making themselves look busy. In proppy or set-ridden shows there is always plenty to do. However, I try to ignore them and we read the first scene together. I notice that some of the men wear pony tails and one has a shaved head and wonder how they can fit into all plays of different periods and surmise that they don't. They probably do one play and are off the rest of the time.

My 'chorus' for *Coriolanus* will be all men, a combination of soldiers, rebels, citizens, servants and messengers. A team will evolve like a corps de ballet and that is what it shall be, as it was in the New York production, the heart and centre of the play. They will be all people at all times and nearly always be on stage. They will be the two armies of Coriolanus and Aufidius. In other words, we will train a team whose strength is increased in relation to the responsibilities they are to carry out and in relation to keeping the 'tune' with each other. The usual. My musician turns up without his instruments. As in England, the director is expected to gas on about his theories for umpteen hours while the cast sit and smoke and ask dumb questions about things that can have no relation to the play since what happens when your adrenalin starts to activate your unconcious is quite different to what you think about when choked full of 'knowledge'.

The musician is asked to bring a drum, at least, to mark out some rhythms and goes out to find one. He's wearing pants cut at the calf and tied by a scarf round his waist. He looks like an 'artiste' and contrasts strongly with my New York musician, Larry Spivak, who looked like a tired overworked tailor and played like a saint. However, time was to prove that first impressions are seldom correct and the musician in Munich proved himself to be every bit as good as Larry.

We read the first scene just to get the feel and then start moving it, piecemeal as it were. I can barely get my lips to open and shut or to motivate across the morning, my mind is in other places. Am I breaking up with my partner? Can I get my new love's face out of my mind? Is she the woman for whom I wish to commit my spiritual suicide? I did the play three years ago in New York with Chris Walken as Coriolanus and Irene Worth as his mother, Volumnia. The chorus was a unit of modern streetwise actors who fused together as a team and then, emboldened with their power and the impression they were making, flew into every scene like greyhounds. The German actors for the chorus look by and large fitter than their American counterparts.

I signal to the drummer to give us the entrance of the citizens. Although he seems too fey to create such a battery of sound, his drum unexpectedly explodes into life. The citizens, crazed with hunger, are about to stage a people's revolution and are rallying together and are even prepared to take on Caius Marcius (Coriolanus) himself. They explode onto the stage as if shot out of a cannon like grapeshot. Freeze. The First Citizen speaks. Their order of movement — action, freeze, dialogue — suggests a highly organised mob that intends to move like a modern dance company or a basketball team, adjusting to each other, quick reactions of head to a word, a sound or any stimuli. Tight-marshalled moves or, as Marcius says, "the many-headed multitude", a mob shaped in a fist. Collective will turned to hate. But the mob, for all their determination, are easily chipped away. Menenius will act as the first break to their surge and with his laborious allegory of the belly makes them sit and listen while he recounts his parable. The mob's locomotion slows and the pulse rate slips a few notches and so softens up for the entrance of Marcius.

The chorus were chosen out of workshops, which they all seemed to like. When I chose the team they seemed a bit miffed and one or two walked out with hurt German pride or actory preciousness since I was picking them as you might cast a chorus line in a musical. I didn't know their names and couldn't be subtle about it, but when the assistant producer asked me who I wanted I had to say, "You, you and you." Anyway, everybody now seems to be in good spirits and enjoying the dive into the deep without the usual day or days long discussion on Roman history . . .

We start to move and the actors throw themselves into it and we detail, plot, twist and turn with the events . . . like a sea swept this way and that by changing winds. The mob fly over the stage, hear distant riots, move in the opposite direction. Shouts, cheers, soul-rending speeches, and run. It already has a good feeling. I start to familiarise myself with the German language. We're in difficulties before we begin. Rufus Beck, who plays Coriolanus, has difficulty with the text, which he complains is wooden and over-rhythmic. In fact the translation is by the 19th-century writer, Tieck. I had always thought of him as a fictional character since I recall Poe's description of the books Roderick Usher read, amongst them "Journey into the Blue Distance by Tieck".

So, for the second time in my life, Tieck raises his spectral head. Rufus feels this version lacks the contemporary feel that a writer with the skills of poet/translator Heiner Müller might have given it. Rufus speaks perfect English and leans over you like a lean hawk and doesn't feel, he confesses, comfortable in the role of Coriolanus. He feels he is more a comedian, mercurial, bizarre, imaginative, whereas Coriolanus is earthbound, rooted, tough and pragmatic. "Someone else should be playing it, someone like *you*." I am flattered and make a mental note to do that very thing as soon as it's feasible . . . I had merely shown him briefly how Coriolanus makes an entrance, real slow, like he was ready to strike back in a flash. Rufus enters too fast and doesn't yet feel his way. So he doesn't get the 'buzz', not yet, but he will.

Menenius, played by our East German actor, comes on and temporises with them and momentarily halts the lava flow of their aggression, enabling it to cool only with tiny spouts still bubbling as individuals question and argue the dialectics of the story . . . Menenius claims the senate is like the belly of the state which must be fed before it can send its energies along the veins of the body to the arms, which are the labour force of the state. It is a neat argument and totally spurious since it is the people who are the stomach and the senate, if anything, is the brain. But Menenius must see things in his own light and since he likes his food and drink the stomach is an appropriate symbol for him. Actually, I don't much like the allegory of the belly since the real body behaves like a perfect communist state, unified and sending the plasma, blood flow and vital minerals through all parts of the body and does not hoard like the stomach unless it wants to be constipated; whereas the senate has the ability to withhold, store and oppress unlike the perfect organism of the body. Therefore, Menenius lies and that is why the people raise their 'arms' against the senate . . . The belly, a big pot belly, no doubt. The rehearsal goes well and the five hours pass without incident. I escape into the summer afternoon.

Sunday 2nd June

Happiness, oh happiness . . . oh Munich. A few tables outside in a back street where cakes are sold in all colours and tastes of the imagination and I have not yet had to face the eruption of a McDonald's or Burger King, like the festering sore on the face of any city (except the cities they were designed for, like the anonymous concrete backwaters of America with its teeming morons). Cafés everywhere, people walking and I have seen no yobs except for the excited crowd that pours into the gargantuan Bierkellers. They pour in in their dozens and occupy giant wooden tables like the ancient beer-swilling peasants from a painting by Breughel or the mess hall of Beowulf . . . but now, along the Leopoldstrasse, all is at peace. The world is quiet . . . not with the death knell that strikes the heart of London on Sundays, except for the markets which are wondrous . . . No, this is not Liverpool either, although the town planners should visit Munich to see how a city functions and, thankfully, I have seen no-one piss in the street, which is becoming a familiar landmark of London after 11pm.

It's been fifteen years since I was last here performing in the Modernes Theatre with my version of *The Fall of the House of Usher* and there is a familiarity, although faint. Bicycles are the preferred mode of transport and many long-legged women are to be seen scything through the streets in thin summer dresses looking quite delicious. Blissful. A couple in their early forties slip out of the house next door to the café where I am contentedly writing. They wheel their bikes out and slowly slide into their familiar day. The man and his woman look attractive, serious, intelligent and represent the new breed of German. Everyone seems to be polite here and no one barfs up in the street.

I've been picking through the works of Edward de Bono; *I Am Right, You Are Wrong* is a good book for those in transit or suffering through the art of creation. His main credo appears to be that 'rock hard logic' is an inherited, non-intuitive and predictable way of looking at life and is the prevalent way of thinking in the West, having "its zenith in Britain" . . . This is in direct opposition to water that adjusts, changes and is mutable. I venture the thought that the barrenness of the theatre scene is in no small way due to 'rock hard logic' being applied and much good work is trampled on. Still smarting from the gruesomely unfair reviews I had in *The Trial*. The sky is perfect today and I visit the little museum called the Villa Stück, which has an exhibition on fakes and there is an interesting film show on movement.

My mind dances with images of the play. Coriolanus enters: I recall Ian McKellen entering, wearing a white lounge suit and carrying a sword over his arm . . . bizarrely the director recruited a kind of Dad's Army for citizens. You were rewarded with the sight of blue-jeaned and sweat-shirted members of the audience pretending to be strikers, whereas the plot calls for gaunt, thin rebels armed with pikes. This seems an example of 'rock hard logic', where one group of rebels in Roman times are meant to be transposed to some teachers' union protesting higher wages. Ian had a rare old go, and was vocally exciting, but he had to shout much of his text over battle scenes and as an actor I know how frustrating that must be. If you cannot be heard you are rendered impotent and some directors seem not to know what an actor has to go through. I hate people tramping around when an actor speaks and having to hear his hard-worked interpretation sullied by the sound of clodhoppers. This is all the more surprising in directors who profess an alleged regard for verse! In the same production I recall Ian's agonising fight with Aufidius which was as unconvincing as it was ill-defined since actors are not by nature warriors or, unless they are a 'Larry', natural athletes. The climax of their meeting, and their much advertised desire to clash, results in many directors thinking, "Oh my God, this has got to be something special", and the poor actors spend many hours with weapons specialists flogging themselves to death. Give me Kirk Douglas.

So you must devise a fight whereby the actor 'acts' the fight since he is a better actor than fighter, so why expose him unnecessarily? So, Rufus comes on and makes his entrance again and still feels miscast since there is such a large fanfare of words building up his aura that any actor, even the most charismatic, will find it hard to live up to the 'image'. The other actors giggle when Rufus makes his speech of contempt to them — they 'know' him as a comedian and his nickname, for what reason I cannot imagine, is 'Mushroom'.

Yesterday we first tried plotting it. When Menenius, who has been entertaining them with his belly parable, says, "Welcome Marcius", since he sees him first, and Marcius says, "Thanks", they slowly turn their heads in unison, and then explode in all directions like a tight group of billiard balls after the white has smashed into them. They don't want to be seen, picked on. Having been softened up by Menenius, their stomach pumps have slowed their adrenalin flow and so they are hardly prepared for Coriolanus' sudden entrance . . . They are frozen like petrified figures at Pompeii. They have exploded to the four corners of the universe, no longer a uniform multi-headed mob. Hiding behind walls, flattened, we imagine in the real situation that Coriolanus is with his storm troops who are surrounding the rebels. The stage is still . . . empty.

It's quiet as an afternoon in Seville or a matinée at the Royal Court. Coriolanus/Marcius steps quietly down, he moves like a mountain cat among chickens, sniffing their fear and deliberating which victim to make an example of, whose skull to crack between his teeth like an eggshell, he's in a killer mood today but deals easily with them . . . walks real slow, like entering a wild west saloon, the sheriff, only he's the fastest draw . . . arrives at the first cowering man . . . very simply . . . "What's the matter, you dissentious rogues, that, rubbing the poor itch of your opinion, make yourselves scabs?" In German it doesn't come out quite so neat. Rufus enters eventually in a long silver grey leather coat and he looks more like a lean wolf than a sheriff or a cat.

We finished rehearsals amidst joy, confusion, anticipation of the next day, excitement over what we have achieved, what scenes to start on Monday and who do we need, and no we can't have him because he's in East Germany finishing his show, and she's at the doctor's, and he's rehearsing something else, and etc., etc. . . . I am now on my way to the English Garden. I glide on the air currents like a bird and walk from Leopoldstrasse through a mini-Arc de Triomphe, where hundreds of second-hand cars are being sold, and into a park the likes of which I could only imagine in my wildest dreams . . .

As if a visitor from another planet or a prisoner released after a long sentence, and deposited in the present world, I wander in complete awe and amazement. Bikes are lined up for hire as you step into the park and you feel this is the escape from the city, the playground and release. Little kiosks serve you your sausages, coffee or ice cream . . . the air is warm and golden and the bike riders slice through the narrow tree-lined avenues. All of a sudden I come into an open area facing onto a narrow river and confront a huge field of sunbathers. Many are starkers . . . not like in Brighton, where a handful of men sit shivering under a grey sky and flashing their new-found freedom on the nude beach (now mostly a gay one) . . . but utterly and completely mixed. Naked men sit or lie in full view of the sun and I must admit that the sight of some trouser-mangled equipment is hardly as edifying as a bush or rainforest dweller whose body is part of and weathered by the environment. Here it looks plain daft. But the men and women of Munich's utterly bourgeois society are claiming freedom from the constraints of the past. And, for a while, verboten is a verboten word, although I must confess that some bloke's scraggy balls staring me in the face is hardly an aesthetic sight.

On the other hand, the women's bodies look healthy and lithe and nobody seems bothered but it is a sight to bring in the tourists. It is also odd to see the Münchners' desire to sit close to each other when there is so much room in the park to spread out; however, it is a testament to the post-hippy German liberation and everybody looks happy. Plus, it is not entirely out of keeping with the pre-war German obsession with health and nature.

In a corner of the park an ambulance stands waiting and its two white-suited medics are sunbathing on two plastic white sheets. Everything in order and no-one will wait bleeding to death while an ambulance is held up in the weekend traffic.

No sooner have I recovered from this blast of freedom-loving flesh than I become enchanted with a fast-flowing river bubbling beneath me as I cross a small bridge; a mini-waterfall in the distance completes the idyllic scene. The trees are dense with bird calls. Then another astonishing sight confronts my wanderlust eyes: a huge Chinese pavilion looms up in the distance, then the giant Tibetan pavilion, which is the showpiece of the park. At least a thousand people, it could be more, encircle the pavilion on wooden chairs around long tables, peacefully, happily, unrousingly enjoying a Sunday afternoon in the sun.

The organisation is perfect — each pavilion has its circular self-service counter, where you choose your fancy from a huge variety of tuck: juicy bratwurst that spit out as your teeth puncture their little fat bodies, spare ribs, frankfurters, chickens, coleslaw, mountains of vegetable salad piled high, wonderful giant pretzels, a Valhalla, an army of citizens fed and wined by the hundreds and no problems. Faces of all nations are there, somehow united by a sense of freedom. Yankees mix easily with German, Italian, Russian, and no horrific oppressive English "time, please" when the cities of England turn into giant urinals and vomitories as the willing masses scoff the last chance saloon before they are shut out. Still banishing those images of grey rotting English life, the released prisoner sees how in all ways restrictions have been lifted here. Now I see more clearly their need for the small flag of freedom in their almost compulsory nudity. Astonishing, for no sooner have I departed from the beer-garden than I find, after a short walk along the shores of a bird-filled lake, another restaurant where I rest my feet . . . at least another 500 or so are seated here. I park at a pink-clothed table where in seconds I am served a mixed salad and a delicious Johannisbeersaft, which is a fantastic redcurrant juice. This is waiter service and everybody is happily chatting away or idly watching the boats going round the lake . . . I sit delirious in the sensations of possibilities not denied and after a while I stroll to the lake where I behold another gigantic café, this time seating another 500 or so sitting by the river and drinking from vast glasses of beer and eating from an equally sumptuous self-service counter. Gargantuan portions of six sausages, spiced and sautéed, served with puréed potato and sauerkraut. To sit in the open air is wonderful when you eat.

Already the park is stunning me but I am growing tired from the wealth of stimulus but can't find the way out. I walk past a children's park with tennis courts and playground and am ready to drop. I rest by the lake, my feet begging for respite. I watch a tiny new-born duck, the most precious thing you could imagine, this tiny ball of fluff creeping round its Mum. I am reminded of Liverpool, where I spent a sour weekend recently, and yet also reminded that the art of the working man, his poetry and songs, most often came from those very simple life styles bordering on deprivation. The fish and chip shop and all-night sausage stand. The grim pub with its workers sinking a pint before going home for egg and chips. The Beatles came from this and for good reason. I walk for hours and eventually find my way out of this demi-paradise. Dinner at the Ischis Café . . . a good pasta and tuna, with a mixed salad and wine. Still outside. Sit and write about my day.

Monday 3rd June

Breakfast at the hotel. What to do? Coriolanus feels inadequate. They say the text is bad and they don't stop complaining about it . . . I've gone off the musician . . . CANCEL!!! This is the only conclusion, and take a hol . . .

cast *Kvetch* . . . who wants to work out with this bunch of complainers? Cancel. You've worked it out in New York so do it yourself in London. Don't waste all this energy on this bunch of cynics. If the lead feels inadequate, then cancel. But first, I will try to make him feel that he is not only adequate but born to play it and if then he doesn't feel right . . .

Wrote sixteen pages yesterday . . . didn't feel lonely for a split second since my writing was my companion. At the next breakfast table I am watching an overweight woman stuffing herself silly, almost perving on it. She wears those loose black clothes so beloved of the overweight that help to create the tent effect. She looks dowdy and grubby as does her partner (male) and from time to time she gives vent to a hacking cough . . . this done with regularity . . . must give her the impression that such a cacophony is the norm . . . I hazard a guess that they might be from the East which has issued a huge exodus in recent weeks with the tumbling of the Wall, that might explain it. My criticism softens and yet, they can't stop eating . . . a beneficence they can't quite believe . . . all this food laid out with such aesthetic skill in the breakfast room. The unfortunate by-product of the Communist system, terrible dowdiness and lack of self-initiative while their spirit is purer than their Western counterparts by far. Now the fat one takes her fags from her grubby handbag. Just before she lights up she gives an involuntary cough of expectation. The Fräulein serving us is a hefty well-built blonde and looks as if she has been through a washing machine, she so radiates a sheen and her blouse is like driven snow . . . The cougher's smoke now weaves its noxious way to my table like the crooked finger of the devil beckoning and now I have to tolerate both her stink and her noise . . . how oppressive some people's mere existence is to others.

Tuesday 4th June

I have to get up really early to avoid the fat, ugly cougher who seems to time her life to disturb me. Still coughing in that kind of 'normal' way like it was a bird sound. The second day goes well . . . The cast are beginning to cohere into an ensemble . . . We run the first small scene, the team sense is developing . . . the cast contradict each other, saying we move on this word or that . . . a self-organising group. When they are interdependent and need to move as a mob, given specific directions and a language of movement, they feel more responsible . . .

Today there are more people 'sitting' round than ever . . . When I came in I saw this army of clerks, the people who sit behind desks and incessantly chatter, it's as if they were going for a picnic and each person has a story to tell: the assistant stage manager talks to the stage manager, and the translator talks to the prompter, and the costume designer is already sitting and watching, and then the dramaturg is checking his translation and it's interesting to hear his suggestions for cuts. For example, when the son of Coriolanus is described by his granny Volumnia, she proudly says, "He had rather see the swords and hear a drum, than look upon his schoolmaster." She beams proudly as if relishing the picture of the future psychopath and how cute, how like Dad. The dramaturg has cut it out as 'stupid' and I have to agree. It is a cloying, sickly love for the cute spoilt kid who tears butterflies apart, and we are meant to find it charming and how like Pa . . . She reiterates, "One on's father's moods", as she glows at his savagery. I detest the fawning over young children's horrible habits just because they are the children of the bosses. I do recall sensing a kind of sickliness when Irene Worth uttered the lines in New York as she paced around our mimed garden with the shears doing her pruning. It suited her and was a piece of business she liked, which suggested the outside world of flowers and butterflies.

I much admired Irene Worth's performance but liked it less when she and Chris Walken would discuss the scene endlessly as if I were not there. I recognised this from 'dead theatre' where the other actors are just feeds for the stars and the leads think the whole play is only about them. I'm not suggesting that Irene thought this, but they were both brought up in that selfish system where directors fawn over their stars and the rest sit in the dressing rooms and wait to be called. This was not the way I worked nor did I like having the poor girl playing the wife, or her friend, having to 'hang about' while the stars sorted it out. Naturally, the stars carry the burden of responsibility and wish to solve their problems but not at the expense of others in their solo spot theatre. It's too easy to recognise this kind of "we build a production around you" theatre. The stars come in and are only terribly concerned about where their entrance and exit is. Their prior employers created nothing out of the material of human flesh and, therefore, the stars came to expect this kind of treatment. I experienced it in the UK as well. I can smell the ravages of neglect, not on the stars but on the mess they left behind. Their serfs. In the end I had to politely request Irene and Chris not to natter so much and we got on with the scene. Thank God, since actor gabble ain't that fascinating and the gabble refuses to let go. It is a way of avoiding doing the scene, as if you have to talk yourself out of it.

Miss Worth didn't speak to me much after that; she is a *grande dame*, a good actress, and is probably used to a bit more fawning. Theatre is a great equaliser, we are all the same. There is no rank in my books or you cannot get moving. Once you genuflect to the star more than their talent deserves, you're in shit street. However, the reviews vindicated me and were unanimous in their praise, giving it merit above the other Shakespeare in Papp's season. I was reminded of this yesterday when Lola came on to do her Volumnia. She is an enthusiastic red-dye-haired lady with a wonderful deep voice sounding curiously not unlike Irene.

Run the first scene again, which is the critical explosion of the cannon at the play's commencement, until Rufus enters and the chorus scatter: split, uptwist, turn, not wishing to be claimed, seen, recognised by the Praetorian Guards. Today, for Rufus as Coriolanus/Marcius, the image is of a fox entering the henhouse. As the chorus run in all directions Marcius stands still and waits. They freeze. He enters . . . slowly, grabs one by the collar and lifts him up with one hand as you might a frightened cat: "What's the matter, you dissentious rogues . . ." Then he drops him, wiping his hands as if sullied by the filthy rags of the plebeians. I like the gesture and the image of a cat with its tail between its legs and remind myself to use it when I play it . . . then I decide against it and resolve not to use anything that Rufus invents but find my own.

This is one of the trials of directing a play that you wish eventually to perform yourself. During the process the director and actor will have invented a mass of ideas and images that you will have to consciously reject, since you feel they have a copyright with the actor. Then you will have to rationalise how much was a joint effort, mutually arrived at through providing the stimulus in the directing, and how much is personal to you as choreographer/director. So a mini-dilemma takes place. I prefer inventing from the beginning so that you are author of your own 'biz'. 'Biz' is the actor's wayward children, the actor's bits of invention that render him at times truly creative and independent from the author and at other times a collaborator.

It also builds up the actor's gallery of identifiable 'moments' . . . Olivier was a master of 'biz' and his death scenes were as much creations as the grand masterpieces of painting.

Rufus now pulls a stick out of one of the rebel's hands and threatens to use it on another. Now the Senators come in and we will have to devise something later that will lift them out of the also-rans. They inform the excited Marcius of the impending war with the Volscians and he responds with joy at the prospect of battling with his old adversary again. The two Tribunes enter next. In the New York production I had one black actor and one white. Joe Papp liked to mix race in the casting and the interesting thing is that after a short period nobody is black or white but just human. Poor Joe died yesterday. I am grateful to have had at least one crack of the New York whip under his historic reign. RIP, Joe.

The Tribunes enter with a slow, shifty gait and the walk seems to express their words, which are furtive, complaining and sneaky. They might walk parroting each other's movements and then split up like two dogs tracking different scents, meeting up again, linking their whining plans and depart. There are no problems and giving each actor a 'physical concept' seems to release them and leave them free to explore the text . . . The actors start to enjoy the slow 'villains' ' walk. The linking in this pair demands that they have a unison and rhythm and so they are busily discussing who starts when. Their walk will be the signature of the Tribunes.

Lola is a full-blooded and bold actress. She will be delightful to work with and enthuses about her scene with Virgilia. She adores the idea of keeping quite still behind Virgilia, who sits, sewing mournfully, in impersonation of Helen. Virgilia mimes the sewing, moving only her arms in Kabuki style. It looks beautiful and serene and creates a delicate visual mantra. I seem to love sewers (people who sew — not the other kind). *Metamorphosis* has the mother sewing, *The Trial* has Mrs Grubach sewing, and now *Coriolanus*. Do women do anything else? For Shakespeare it is as if women must be seen to be doing something domestic and restrained. And so, Virgilia sews her invisible web and her friend Valeria will be obliged to say "A fine spot, in good faith" while the chappies tear people or butterflies apart.

The theatre canteen: I enjoy theatre canteens in Europe since they usually reflect the bottom line of earthy local working-class food. This one is no exception, it's greasy spoon nosh, German style. Huge plates of food are handed out, decked with mashed, creamy potatoes, sliced meats, or mince, and oodles of gravy, full of taste. Although meat is the staff of the German people, it still amazes me what a vast consumption of animal takes place. Tons of meat flow along the kitchens of the Bierkellers along with lakes of Löwenbräu. This canteen is serviceable and functional and seats twice as many as the one at our little National Theatre, although the NT has good grub.

I can't eat during rehearsals and so I peer over and admire the giant partitioned plates with separate areas for salad and veg. I feel quite cosy in here and am treated brusquely by the old Bavarians running it; their method is to tolerate you and then eventually spoil you . . . It's been two days and I feel I have had enough, working five-hour sessions with breaks for coffee.

In the mornings I love to run in my local park, which is an extension of the English Garden. The path I have worked out takes me around the statue of the mad King Ludwig four times. The run lasts about 20 minutes and puts me in a serene mood.

Start rehearsals with Volumnia and Virgilia and decide to have them both sewing in unison, sitting on their chairs.

The composer has created some ravishing marimba music for the scene and so it is beautiful before the women even open their mouths. Lola is a delight to work with, as is Sona MacDonald, and I spend the morning doing Marceau-style impersonations of a butterfly since I want Valeria to reflect this with her hands the way one does when one tells the story. But the actress is taking a long time to loosen those leaden wings so unused to flight. However, I love working with the easiness of the female members of the cast who, among the company, are the only ones to freely express their delight at playing with gestures and using their own bodies.

We actually work for about an hour or so and then the 'chaps' come in and I suddenly feel oppressed, working with nine men. I knew I still had the first stages of the battle scene to work out. Since Marcius talks about horses I will take this as an invitation to have the company riding in on mimed stallions, rising slowly and majestically up and down, a kind of stylised physical shorthand.

The riders actually come on during the ladies' sewing circle or, more precisely, when Virgilia is left sewing. As she sits there in the garden, wistfully weaving her embroidery, a drum cracks into life and the horses enter and surround her — much like a film, which takes us from her thoughts to her son and missing husband, to the battlefield. The garden is obliterated by a display of macho muscle: all talk of butterflies, children, sewing, is trampled underfoot by male domination. Am I trying to crush out my own feminine side which flowed so easily with the women in order to assert my masculine power? Through a need that, while adoring the female, the lyrical, sensual, soft, fluttery butterfly, I must perforce demonstrate my allegiance with 'the lads'? So, protesting that I am not really a butterfly but a strong male, I am trying to re-emerge into the world of men. Escape from Mum's influence.

The horses are now on and riding. I commence the battle. I might in the past have attempted to choreograph a series of moves to demonstrate a battle sequence but, as a legacy from New York when Chris Walken was always so impatient to move on and get his 'overview', I sketch the battle out briefly. And it works. So, instead of a routine which might have taken weeks to perfect, we invent a free-for-all in three short bursts of frenzied activity. It is an explosion of ten seconds of highly energetic movement followed by an abrupt halt, with the heavy breathing in the still period giving the taste of the battleground. The stillnesses are the key. The exhaustion, the heaving and panting, being utterly drained and then, as the drums crack, renewed effort, and the subsequent exhaustion growing — until after a few bursts the actors are in a state of collapse. So, we go from fit and strong to listless and debilitated. Thus we act the battle rather than impersonate it. Rufus watches at first, as did Chris, as if the General were keeping an eye on the battle. But he eventually joins in and leads the affray; with his exhilarating sense of movement he makes an impressive display.

I can sometimes feel too aware of a presence in the room, of a friend or visitor who watches. Today, quite naturally, the costume designer is in and watching. I had a working dinner with her last night. I felt like having female company in this city, instead of my usual solitary repast. By the act of eating together we established a greater intimacy. There was a certain exposure to the map of my life. As a result I am more keenly aware of her presence here now. She has a greater claim on my being than the others and has charted further down the Amazon of my nervous system. I feel exposed and oppressed and strangely wish her gone. I feel unfree and yet soldier on and feed instructions to my brain: "Ignore her presence." But she knows me as a human being with senses, feelings and an ability to bleed. I am not a figure called her director any more. Eventually I absorb it into my system and carry on.

Rufus is turning into a mercurial firework and now gets into the swing of playing a psychopath and releasing that murderous energy with his voice: he achieves a new crystalline clarity, his young elastic vocal cords screaming out room-shattering shrieks. In my private tormented mind I compare my voice to his and reassure myself that I can do this too when I am warmed up. I know that in releasing his voice he will break open those locks that keep the demon in. As a director I will not be able to shout, scream, lose myself; and so his growing power will be in contrast and opposition to my administrative power which, although considerable, has yet to be restrained and marshalled. I have an army of thoughts under my banner and yet one free radical dancing about can obscure and unfocus me. I am suddenly jealous of this freedom and am in competition with Rufus. I am no longer 'Herr Direktor' but an actor with no chance to avenge myself; yet I am, and must be, pleased with him. He has found himself and I am forced to *watch*. The adrenalin courses into his brains. I break for coffee and *need it*.

I sit with two chaps and we natter slightly. One tells me of a Canadian director, Robert Lepage, who had done *A Midsummer Night's Dream*, which he saw. I retort tartly, "He's always doing it!" since I had expressed a desire to create a *Dream* at the National with myself as Oberon and Richard Eyre mentioned that Robert Lepage was doing it for them. An actress in *The Trial*, whom I directed recently at the National, also spoke of a very inventive *Dream* she had seen in Canada and so I felt this must be his calling card. One of the actors, Wolfgang Bauer, who has his head shaved like a punk, says, "When did you last do *Coriolanus*?" Touché. "Only once." Actors are watching beasts and don't let anything slip by them. Nine of them watching you in rehearsal. Nine pairs of eyes taking you apart and dissecting you piece by piece, quick to spot your weaknesses.

Rufus keeps chatting to the cast in German while I stand by, unable to follow at that speed, feeling helpless, without a rudder to guide me over the lake which is Germany. I think it devious to be able to use a secret code which any language must be when it is unfamiliar. Then I am left waiting in the dark so to speak and cannot really say "Come on, guys . . . use my lingo." Rufus is always concerned with his 'image' — what he looks like or sounds like — and tends to fuss rather than work it through. He will show his displeasure if we sketch through a scene, and pout or look fed-up even though it seems to work. It may be that he is dissatisfied with himself. He's a star of the company and does take himself quite seriously, a touch trendy. For rehearsal he wears his own calf-length elegant boots and a raincoat plus a small bandana round his forehead, while his streaked blond/ash hair shoots out like ears of corn.

I turn my attention to the problem of creating the 'gates of the city'. Most directors put a huge pair of gates onstage and have the soldiers surging through them when they open. For the New York production I had the actors rushing through one of the exits downstage into the auditorium and out and in this way the audience imagined that the gates were offstage. Here we cannot do that and so I need to create a pair of gates, but symbolically. Well, we resort to the tried and true mime figuration whereby two actors become the gates. The gates are about resistance and so the two actors' arms become the resistance. The cast fling themselves against the invisible area of the great gates and push. Eventually the arms 'open'. Then the two gates turn into the soldiers pouring in. Not only is it effective, it gives the audience an 'idea' rather than a reality. It works well and looks interesting and the gates are dissolved. Eventually the day is over and the actors are convinced, though rather mystified, that the gates work. It is the imagination that likes to work and supplies the missing ingredient. I am relieved. I am not yet enamoured of this company and find myself continually commanding "Quiet, please", since they are always yacking and seem to lack professional discipline. The new era of communal co-operation. Rufus is a bit of a comedian and he has the habit of interrupting when I am showing something to someone else and yet soon complaining about the lack of time we have to complete the show. He is a bit prima-donna-ish but is a good actor though suffering from a surfeit of ego. He even writes out his own translation.

Wednesday 5th June

A bit down in the dumps and I seriously consider leaving though I know I won't. I don't like the idea of spending a month looking at these actors. Apparently Günther has not gone down too well with the burghers of Munich since his arrival from Düsseldorf (where I first worked with him) and he has been much criticised for his productions. Possibly he is too smart and urban for them and is prone to take too many risks which is out of character for the staid 'Residence Theatre'. Günther is a slim, jet-setting cultural swinger who spends much of his time in Eastern Europe. I imagine he feels the theatre is either rougher or more vital there or he has some tinge of remorse for his privileged position in the West. He also loves going to Israel and brings Jewish companies to Germany. The Germans also go there! His voice has a tendency towards a high-pitched tone and I mentally cast him with his steel-cropped modern hairstyle and blue eyes as the cultured but benevolent Nazi in my manual of German types. He manifestly is not a Nazi and could not ever be — anyway Nazi is beside the point; I am thinking only of race and personality, and the Nazi Party, with its uniforms, correctness, mania for cleanliness and phobia about strangers was a collective squeezing of the German character into its essence. That the essence was poisoned by the Nazi machine is indisputable but there does exist here an intense obsession with law and order — although seeing Munich on Sunday they seemed to be a freer, happier society. However, I could not help but think about how they were all so obsessed with my extremely modest hotel allowance, all quoting "It's the law", the same way as hiding behind duty. Still, they are much more generous in their payments for work done as a director than they could ever be in Britain and you can also enjoy the fruits of your labour in the wonderful cafés of Munich.

This is my stern-faced waitress with her puffed-out pleated skirt and strong shoulders, bound by a tight bra across her muscled back and seen in my mind's eye with a whip striding the long avenues of Dachau. These thoughts are not so easy to budge, especially when I see her hard, scrubbed face; however, here she is, thankfully harmless, and serves coffee and not lashes. Everyone in the breakfast room smokes and coughs.

Günther tells me that the cast don't know what's going on. How am I going to direct: what period, style, form, character? I quite forgot to tell them! I just started rehearsing and imagined that by showing them and by example they would soon see, rather than hear theories spouted out of my gob for six hours. I thought — wrong! They can't see. They need to sit and be bored for endless hours rather than benefit from seeing in practice. Also I never presume to know in advance what might happen in rehearsal, or that the combination of elements might produce another effect to the one I imagined in advance. Theatre is a physical act. We move and feel, not just talk. I had in fact discussed the formation of the citizens and soldiers as chorus, and the moving structure of the play. The set and environment are key witnesses to the struggle, participate as an ever-changing mask for each scene.

I have a theory that the actors like the ritual of being talked to, of having the director sit there and obeying the ritual. They want what is the norm and feel used and frustrated. They wish to be participants at a lecture and be pandered to, no matter how revolting this is in practice when demonstration on the spot is far more valid. Also, is there a whinge factor that makes them seek out the Daddy to complain to like whining children with no inner guts or conviction? Has subsidy so rotted their spines — combined with the anti-Nazi over-liberal element — that any form of authority is suspect, even if it's in artistic conviction? I never heard such continuous moaning in my life. The production is destined to be a success.

I am still dipping into, on my rare opportunities, my Edward de Bono book and find that his theories are almost a blueprint for the theatre. Those whose minds can weave like water and those whose minds are stiff as rocks. Now, within this group I have assembled scattered individuals into a formidable power that seems even greater than their collective strength. Now, quite normally — and it's satisfying to watch — they are starting to think and perform like a body. They suggest, remember for each other, correct and adjust as if the body were repairing its own wounds.

As I have said, and I only repeat it since this is the first impact of the play and in a way its code for the rest, the entrance of the citizens, exploding on to the stage as if they had been vomited out of the mouths of the angry city, is very forceful. A cynical mob, a questioning mob, an angry frightened mob, in fact a mirror image of society: a multi-headed multitude. It's so clear, and the body language further amplifies the text. Now, having done this, the request to explain what I have done seems an act of perversity. It's like describing a meal your guest has just eaten. It is a perversity that is beyond human belief. The play is going forward with leaps and bounds and I can see the relish in the performers, but the need to whine, whinge and complain seems so much a part of this company's character, and it is reflected in the German nation as a whole. I noticed this in Düsseldorf when doing *The Trial*: anything that doesn't have the ABC of plodding naturalistic familiarity and the linear thinking of the plodder is invalid; Narcissus confronting himself in the mirror, the actor's desire to express himself as the centre of the universe rather than as a member of a society and group, as a member of the human race with its familiar patterns. So in Düsseldorf they again went to the Herr Intendant and whined like kids in a kindergarten.

Somebody has just brought to my attention a German newspaper review of *The Trial*, which is very bad. So the filthy scumbag of a journalist thought he would try to trash me while I was attempting to create a memorable *Coriolanus*. Some Schweinhund who thinks Kafka is German has decided to poison the atmosphere with a scurrilous little fart of a review. Now, while this is unimportant, what is significant among this gang of wallies is that two of them rushed up to Günther's office to show him the review! With some characters, and I've come across some, one is sorely tempted to give in to historical prejudice. I could not begin to describe the sheer awfulness of the productions I have seen here, to give colour to their sublime ugliness and perverted theatre. And yet these clowns go running around like slimy Nazi informers; there, I have said it, but nothing else seems a suitable epithet for them. The sexual repression that forces them to attempt to deny it by tearing their clothes off on stage or simulating acts of sex in front of the concerned liberal cabbages that sit out there watching this trash. Now, on reflection, even their determined stripping down to the buff, with their ugly porky white bodies, seems less like an act of liberation than a misguided effort to peel themselves from the skin of the bourgeois stultification which strangles them as soon as they leave the park.

So I am summoned to Günther's large white office, and once again he invites me to the house. Yeah, perhaps next week when you return from the last performance of *The Trial*, as I am still acting in that, and this is my week off from the National Theatre. Anyway, next week, when I return.

In the meantime I will spend from 5pm onwards not talking to a soul until rehearsal next day. My system seems to have broken down somewhat and since I have been here I have been aided by pills. My stomach is the first to react to any stress, so while Menenius says the senate is the stomach, I could say my stomach is the battlefield, and my bowels turn to concrete. I seriously thought this morning of leaving. Doing an Ivor Pogorelich — my concert-playing friend of Clara's is always cancelling or quick to walk out if conditions go against his better judgement. I go to bed early and switch on the TV. Hear the oily voice of CNN. The American news pitches everything with that syrupy optimism and nasal tones, such normality posing behind the decent masks of regularity. The Dow Jones Index: "Buying has been bullish", and we cut to scenes of half a dozen rotten yuppies manning half a dozen telephones; then to the Middle East and Muslim fanatics being predictably fanatical; then to Africa to see babies looking like dehydrated monkeys; and finally to Bush, mouthing more platitudes than flies around a piece of dogshit. Of course, there's no news from the UK.

Thursday 6th June

It's hard work and my heart is not in it. Our Coriolanus is too wild at the moment, with his flaying limbs. The woman's perfume stinks at the breakfast table. Why do women have to stink like whores when they come down to breakfast? I've had enough and need a holiday badly. My guts ache and I'm too much alone. Germany has always meant loneliness to me. I hate working on the play and don't know how to endure it. Four more weeks of concrete stomach.

I start with the butterfly scene again, as the little son is described tearing it to pieces in his rage against something beautiful. The actress moves like cement. I can't bear actresses who have no sense of their bodies; when Sona does it she looks wonderful. Too much realism and taking their clothes off and simulating fucking. Yes, they're good at that, but try and give the impression of a butterfly and you're lost and swimming in shit. We're into the scene of the horses again, which now is improving and they're looking good. The battle's good: there's a rush off stage and "the gates are open". Of course I resort to the mimed gates, as described, with the two men, but am I falling into repeating my own conventions? The 'gates' today don't look so good any more and Coriolanus' fight against an invisible foe also looks less good — but we need a scene before the mob comes back and this fills in nicely. We cut as if in film to Coriolanus slashing his way through an army of flesh, or so we hope it appears. The soldiers return, weary after their battle offstage, and Coriolanus returns bloody but unbowed to woo them to fight once more. We go into the slow-motion killing, where every aspect of death on the battlefield is shown in all its gruesome glory. A man steps out into the darkness, illuminated by a single shaft of light when, coming up behind him, and slowly, is his Nemesis. The first man is despatched and the second slowly moves in the swirling fog until a third man comes up and despatches him, and so on until all are writhing on the floor, oozing out their precious life, sliding and rolling slowly over, like turf being unfolded. Then we see Coriolanus despatch the last one and also move away until he confronts Aufidius. So, by this process, we are able to see how the events of battle lead Coriolanus into the arms of Aufidius and we have almost broken down the first act. It's getting better and my spirits are rising. Rufus has a controlled energy now and he explodes and dives into the maelstrom — though he must keep something in reserve.

The Assistant Director comes along with my first cheque. This is the first third and is already equivalent to my National Theatre fee. The first week is down and I must fix what we have. Let them run this during my absence: fix music, moves, etc. Don't need more battles! Let's get back to the play. I don't wish to direct any more; exhaustion, weariness, fatigue, sense of diminishing power. Just act!

Friday 7th June

Went to bed early last night after a spaghetti al fresco at Café Roma. People alone are treated like lepers: the waiter can hardly bring himself to attend to you. The pasta was good though, and I ate it with pleasure, watching the tramcars sliding past with the bleary faces of their occupants staring out. Germany can make you feel a little like an insect if you are not part of it. Nobody asks what you do to amuse yourself at night. They put it out of their minds, as if you had lived there all your life. You carve out what small comforts you can. Nobody phones to see if you are sitting alone with a plate of spaghetti. So the night I arrived was a fluke, when we all went for a pasta at this same café and, being a guest, I paid my share. The week has drifted away and my ulcer hurts daily from some kind of unresolved stress and tension. Watching the cynical faces of the cast if I falter or seem unsure, stumble a bit, but up to now the play looks good. With our limited cast, where the chorus serves a multiple functioning, utilitarian group, would there be difficulty in telling the good guys from the bad guys? Would it get confusing? In the first battle we only see the army of Coriolanus, fighting the enemy, and see by their attacks who they are killing — since the enemy is invisible and they are, in one sense, miming the opposition. We show conflict and attack and don't need the obvious men facing men. The insane explosion of activity after the whiplash of the drum works well, as it did in New York. On the last percussion, and the last feeble effort to fight, Marcius comes on and literally pulls them together, dragging the separate parts from all areas of the stage to make one mound of flesh; then, having put together his octopus of heaving, breathless bodies, he leaps on to their backs like a chariot-rider. He rails at them and whips them beyond their strength and into their reserves. They become recharged and renewed as they pile into the gates. Again, the 'gate' scene bothers me and we cut it and just charge offstage: after all, we do say "the gates are open". I recall the Berliner Ensemble's huge gates in their revolving set but I would like to use our symbol of one, if I am going to use it at all. It works well since, as they go through the gates, they turn and we 'see', if you like, the reverse side as they enter the city.

Dreamed last night of the sea and boats and was momentarily at peace. When I woke I was horrified to think I had to face the mob again: those healthy, strapping, cynical blokes. Do I have a complex with their young male physical strength? Am I jealous since they are of an age with my present heart-breaker? However, I am getting over it. They may be the machine but I am the brains behind the whole enterprise. I still debate with myself. I dreamed I shot, for no good reason, someone called Mr King, a kind of politician. I shot him through my TV set and in the dream it appears I did it on behalf of Ian McKellen. Now, apart from the dream, how's this for synchronicity? I was hoping to go back to London one day earlier in my first shift of rehearsals and decided to make up a story that Tony Sher, who is playing Joseph K. in *The Trial* at the National Theatre, was ill and that of course we'd need to rehearse. Last night, when ringing home, I was informed that Sher had been struck by appendicitis and is going to be off work! Ye gods, I prophesied it! I have already packed all my bags in case I never come back but I decided to try and make it easier for myself.

Don't work with the chaps all day, since it's so wearying; just do two hours and work the other scenes. There's plenty of others to work out. Take more days off and even do a four-day week! Like this week. The first weeks are always the worst . . . I haven't even learned their names yet and I should learn them all, that will help. Last Sunday was a revelation of sun and joy but today is real Munich: grey, wet, drizzly, uniform buildings, long straight streets and Bierkellers.

My system has partly broken down and my sewage is aided by detonating explosive charges in the shape of little pills which seem to do the job. It is with gratitude that I feel the urge to 'open the gates'. How your stomach or your bowels are is a barometer of your wellbeing. At home, where I am well fed and cared for in body and spirit, I function like a factory — but working with dear Chris Walken (who off-stage is a gem) and in *The Prisoner of Rio*, a compost heap of a film that came and went or died, have been the only times my system has broken down, rebelled and needed help. I read that 100,000 have died from AIDS in the USA. Probably mostly young men. What a waste of life. Twice the casualties of the Vietnam War. I suddenly think of my New York *Coriolanus* team, my great black Aufidius, of Keith David and my friendly team of players. Must avoid too much slow motion. Mind you, the way we do it is the best on earth.

[P.M.] Hooray! I'm on a Lufthansa on the way to London. The manner of the German girl on the desk is appalling if your ticket is not quite so, doesn't fulfil every scintilla of clerical requirements. My stomach ache cleared up and my run put me in a better mood. Sweated freely and ran six times round King Ludwig the Second. The rich, full-grown trees were heavy with their foliage and old ladies walked their dogs. Nobody else was running. I was so relieved to be on top again after feeling as if the weight of the world was on me. Woke up after a pleasant dream which soon evaporated, leaving bands of sweat on my forehead when I faced the realisation that I must rehearse with them today. But they really are nice lads. Quite an unusually good-looking lot, which must have something to do with Günther's taste. After all, the audience must be visually entertained as well. The public like to see virile pretty guys on stage. It was raining when I walked past a familiar building on the way to work. It looked a washed-out colour, like strawberries that had been out in the rain for a week. Rufus had been to the dentist and couldn't speak for a couple of hours so we did the slow-motion battle with Aufidius, and the dozen stage managers, translators, dramaturg, designer and prompter all watched how elegantly their director moved. Aufidius has never understood his body but makes a brave attempt and in an hour's break actually goes for a haircut to make himself look 'tough'.

Saturday 15th June

So it is just over a week later and in that miserable little week I have done nothing to change the world, merely repeated habits. Continued with Titorelli and all four performances were in good form. I have never enjoyed a character so much: I am so released in it and now, with the breath under control, it flows like a dream. Alan Perrin took over from Tony Sher, now in hospital, and did very well indeed — in fact his characterisation was much admired by all.

While auditioning for my play *Kvetch* I actually developed a kvetch over one of the auditioner's voices and attack: I felt he was a powerful actor and would he compete with me? I have to admit it gave me a mite of concern but then again, when you're sitting down watching everyone else act, they all seem better than you because you are not doing it yourself. It's alright, since volume isn't the criterion but it's obviously one of my bugbears of the past where I felt vulnerable: a stong voice seems to symbolise power and danger. This is not always true, it can also suggest yards of boredom. It depends how it's used. Well, the actor blasted out and it was a powerful explosion, and I winced, thinking, "How can I follow that?" and I had to convince myself that I wouldn't be prejudiced if I didn't choose him and asked the two stage managers what they thought of him. Both said, unaware of my feelings, that he wasn't really right for the part, which he wasn't. (We chose instead an actor who really gave me a run for my money as it turned out: Henry Goodman.) The volume and blast man was too old and set in his ways. Thank God for that. I would have taken him on had it been otherwise, kvetch or no kvetch. In a mood of vocal paranoia, when I played

Titorelli in the evening, I was hyper-aware of Perrin's sharp metallic ring and made a conscious effort to increase the dial on my inner volume control without losing the 'colour'. The next night I forgot all about it and concentrated on the colours and humour and everything worked perfectly for the matinée and evening.

Between shows I had coffee in Covent Garden with a chap who wants to work with me on a screen version of the famous Yiddish folk story about exorcism, *The Dybbuk.* Sona MacDonald, who is playing Virgilia in Munich, actually flew to London to see *The Trial* and was much taken by the production. Of course, this must make for good propaganda when she gets back to Germany and tells the disgruntled and suspicious cast. That all seems a long way away now. We went upstairs to the National Actors and Staff bar and it was packed with the actors from *The White Devil*, now rotting like a corpse in the Olivier. Since I am not on until the second act in *The Trial* I sometimes cock an ear to what the others are doing and hope to while away a pleasant hour but so far I haven't been able to take more than fifteen minutes. It became an endurance test. I hated sitting alone in my dressing room but it seemed the lesser of the two evils. I watched fifteen minutes of incomprehensible drivel, rendered even more muddy by an elaborate set that dominated everything. And the text was woolly. I felt for the assembled mass of heads sitting obediently still like coconuts on shies, dutifully looking at this and trying to hold on to the belief that they were watching culture. I felt sad for all their efforts in dressing up, buying tickets, getting babysitters, parking cars, depleting their incomes and getting bored and frustrated in the process. I am always glad to crawl back to my dressing room when I see what passes for drama. The last night came and I ran the scene before going on and had a momentous angst about a word, which is likely to happen, because it's the final hone. However, I solved it, and we celebrated with a few drinks upstairs. Nobody from management came to see the final show with Alan Perrin brilliantly taking over the lead role. So here was an actor of the first rank, taking over the reins at short notice, and nobody took a blind bit of notice. I did receive a nice card from Richard Eyre, expressing regret that he couldn't come to the party. Our party was successful and it was OK that nobody from the National management came; after all, like all large institutions, this is a factory theatre where too many children beg for attention.

It's a warm day in Munich and I crawl out of bed and brave the breakfast lounge. It's full of yacking people and a middle-aged bald Yankee is whining in a voice of anal retention, "Do you have any liverwurst this morning?" I can't take it and quickly fill a plate with some oversweet muesli, take a tray and eat it in peace on my terrace. I walk to work and idly wonder what's in store today and try to shrug off some unwelcome thoughts I have dragged over from London. When you work, act or direct you must do it as if your life depended on it: I read this from the mouth of Boris Becker and it's no less true for me. Your life at this time is expressed through your work and what you think, feel, know, desire and hope for is expressed therein. I turn into the yard of the Prince Regent Theatre and it looks just as I left it a week ago. The small fountain is still trickling away and I stop to stare into the water, perhaps hoping that some small silvery fish might glide past and calm my turbulence.

I open the door knowing that the cast would have begun at 11am since today they must finish at 4pm as one of them has a show at 8pm and must have the mandatory four-hour rest. I said I would begin at noon, working with some scenes that I left off last week. As I come in I open the door a crack and see the usual army of people sitting behind desks and hear a lot of talk and wonder what scene they are running. I suddenly can't face it and think of going away until my appointed time since there is still half an hour to go. Then I decide, "What the hell, let's try and concentrate", and walk in, smiling and saying hello to everyone. "Carry on", I say, hoping they will continue their scene but they are all yacking on about how hard done by they feel and one actor after another makes his point. The text is a 'problem' (their favourite word) and how in Germany the director sits down and describes his method or point of view; how he 'sees' the play and characters, what the purpose is. The psychology, period, atmosphere, blah, blah, blah! They feel I have not let them into the secret, that in jumping in I haven't described the journey they would take, etc., etc.

I see how they need to avoid and evade the purpose of doing it, embracing the age-old constipation that takes no risks but stores it all up and questions all intuition, daring or experiment with long boring discussions which have no relevance to the play and, in fact, would prevent the free flow from taking place. I tell them that I have sat watching countless boring productions of Shakespeare where the director had come armed with his hours of notes and 'homework' . . . that I describe the play in the doing of it. You jump in the water and in that way you determine the temperature. I add that what we have done already is exciting and has meaning and they shouldn't separate form and content since the form is the interpretation.

I can see them trying to retain the dead structure of the old world order with their need for explanations when, in fact, it *is* as clear as the hand before your face. I had a theory that it was very simple and that they wanted it to be complicated and had an unconscious desire to sabotage what was flowing all *too* easily. Our army of citizens, who were soldiers and chorus, already defined the concept of the play which was to liberate the actors from the static role of bourgeois representationalism with one man per role and a mirror image of life. It was already clear to those who connect themselves to society and do not see themselves as strutting egos with their little 'characters'. The structure so far would be clear to children, who automatically connect with each other, and would see no problem in what we were doing. The text is clear and now they must show *me*, based on what the text says. The play describes a fascist regime in whatever climate we wish, whether under Mussolini, Hitler or whatever comes to mind, but we were heading towards Italian. I stage-manage the events and the actor must trust his own devices. I collect all their views but do not forget to add that everybody's background is different and everybody will interpret my lectures according to their own mind-set. The doing is all. These actors were, unconsciously, already impersonating the disgruntled plebs begging for my corn, the multi-headed multitude, except that instead of corn they wanted attention and knowledge when it was in themselves to acquire it by practice. In fact they were denying themselves their own intelligence and wanting to be led by a Führer who tells them how to think. But they keep on whining and I am getting sick of them and their constant use of the word 'problem'. I say that by using that word they make a problem with their negative feedback.

Eventually we start from the beginning and it turns into a full-heated and exciting rehearsal and we make many new discoveries, including a marvellous rhythmic fresco as the battle continues while Aufidius makes his speech of pain at being defeated by Coriolanus in single-handed combat. After all the rubbish talk the cast now work and move as if they know exactly what to do and what is expected of them. I try to concentrate and get through the day without taking a single break for myself and go from scene to scene. Now I am relieved to have finished reworking each scene in my mind. It was more exciting than any Shakespeare I have seen but then again I'm prejudiced. I have a late lunch in the English Garden with the designer and go home early to bed.

Late at night I watch the CNN news and see the world divided into a kind of smorgasbord as the chewing-gum voices of the newscasters turn the people into play-school with its naughty interruptions as one nation after another goes about murdering or starving, but in the same oily nasal happy tones, their voices reducing the gravity of what they are saying into local nuisances. Thus a train shot up in India by the Tamil Tigers is read out like the weather forecast, more storm than expected. The Philippine disaster, where a volcano has erupted with dire results, is really weird and we keep seeing the same old duffer shuffling along in the ashen mud with a face crossed between utter bewilderment and hopelessness, and yet the effect is mitigated by his cap, one of those yankee-style baseball caps which now cover the bonces of the world. Every hour, when the news comes on and the sky turns black, we see the same shot of the little old man shuffling along his muddy black street, his life appearing as meaningless and pointless as a character out of Beckett; we watch all this from the luxury hotels of the world that are advertised on CNN. So now this little old man, covered in filth and lice, on the muddy black road, is a 'star'; everyone in America seems to talk in headlines, clichés and homilies . . . The floats are now celebrating the welcome home of the Iraqi War soldiers. Baby talk is prevalent, a kind of nursery babble . . . Now we're discussing the 'drrrurggs warr', which is the current mantra of America: how they deal with drugs when, in fact, they encourage it. Free enterprise is a reaction to poverty and a health service which costs a fortune unless you wait in long queues, so if medicine can be as expensive as any drug, you may as well sell drugs to obtain it!

Now there is a programme on bats to demonstrate to children that they are not vampires but beautiful creatures, and there was a travelling exhibition to re-educate children which, in fact, it did. And then the idiot newsreader, in direct contradiction to the whole thrust of the programme, which is to deracinate the old hoary prejudice, says, "Creepy". With one word she entirely negates what the programme set out to do. Just to show she is not a congenital moron but a nice soft lady who squeals at the 'creepy' bits in movies. Then we see Bush and Reagan strongly denying that they had traded missiles for hostages. Bush says, like any old gangster in a 'B' movie, that he'd welcome an investigation as long as it didn't cost a billion dollars, thus posing as the standard-bearer of values. The defenders of the 'red-cent of the taxpayers', note the Huckleberry Finn pattern, the American family friend and White House Norman Rockwell figure who weeps for our boys while calmly allowing one million Kurds to meet their end! Ronnie in his family doctor spiel also resorts to candy simplicity: "We just want to bring them home." Home: like he was Dad at the fireplace waiting for our boys as he poses for the Rockwell cover. John Major says he wants to re-unite the hostages with their families, a far more distinctive description of the events.

Next we are exposed to a screaming harridan teaching an aerobics class and a lot of fat ugly women pretending to be Jane Fonda. So, between being induced to eat at Burger King, they are being blackmailed to sweat it off at an aerobics class until they go into a coma; and between all this there is nothing to help them recover their minds like a spot of culture! There is no news on any culture whatsoever in theatre, arts, literature, nothing in performance except Kevin Costner in that ghastly shit, *Robin Hood.*

Yankeeland destroys culture as if it were a dangerous virus and the great minds of yesteryear are seldom performed at all. In the end culture is a mulch for soft molars. I recall the ghastly fur coats pouring out of their limos to see Mischa in *Metamorphosis* on Broadway, and equally the mulch-conditioned 'subscribers' walking out of the same play dressed in blue blazers and white pants made of recycled polystyrene and whose longest word is 'validated parking'. Give the bums Neil Simon, who is a worthy writer, and *Tally's Follies*. Mind you, they didn't go a bundle on poor Kenneth Branagh and his Shakespearean touring show but he did get it to LA, which shows that contacts are as valuable as talent (if not more).

An interview on CNN. Bush has supported the regime of this villain in El Salvador. Two lap dogs for CNN pretend to do an in-depth interview but succeed in cleaning up his bloody hands. The two 'journalists', and I am using that word advisedly, are called Evans and Novak. They briefly raise the question of the murders of the Jesuit priests (six!) and then tacitly suggest in their new 'CNN-speak' that Castro be Saddamised! Is this news or shit . . . ? They end up praising the President of El Salvador for his coolness! Or maybe they are being ironic, suggesting that if the villain achieves peace he should get the Nobel Peace Prize!

Sunday 16th June

Yesterday we finished with the scene of Volumnia meeting Menenius with the tidings of joy of Coriolanus' home-coming. Our Menenius comes from East Germany where in the theatre everything is discussed, debated and analysed for weeks before one even begins to plot the play. Menenius has even learned the text. The benefit from his side is that he has done his research and homework and has arrived at his own conclusions for the character and is perfectly attuned to whatever direction I wish the play to go. He is the most malleable of them all and gives a thorough, clean and straightforward rendering of the text. He sits patiently, waiting for his scene and has no 'problems' or even queries. He seems to understand perfectly what I desire from the scene and even is in accord with it.

We tried to create the great excitement Volumnia generates with her 'news' . . . Menenius is of course delighted to see his own class after the dreary, whingeing Tribunes and his enthusiasm expresses itself volubly. The girls enjoyed doing the scene and it made a change to work again with such positive and enthusiastic people. Perhaps it is the young who always have a dilemma. They wish to destroy Zeus.

The scene before with the Tribunes was way overlong and we have trimmed much of it. I felt that it was a time-waster, put there to allow a realistic passage of time to elapse before we see Coriolanus appear after announcing his imminent arrival. The main points are put over and that is that. Menenius sees his beloved Marcius as a victim of the people (big joke) while the Tribunes rightly see the reverse side of the coin. We all write from the point of view of our present attitudes to our times and reflect the present time even if it is hidden behind the mask of antiquity. Of course, Shakespeare, being an aristocrat of letters, viewed the plebs as an illiterate bunch, concerned mainly with bread and booze and not the stuff of heroes and kings. I feel the plebs for him are what north-country yokels were for our Edwardian playwrights: simple, good-natured folk, easily led and easily roused, while the aristocracy were the true leaders of taste and quality, education and power, an attitude seeming to find new life in this country at the moment. The corn riots in the play were taken from a contemporary event and Shakespeare points to a very strong case for an aristocracy based on virtue and power when Coriolanus says, debunking democracy as practised by the Greeks: ". . .when two authorities are up, neither supreme, how soon confusion may enter 'twixt the gap of both and take the one by the other." Also his contempt for the rights of the people: ". . .where gentry, title, wisdom cannot conclude, but by the yea and no of general ignorance, — it must omit real necessities." No, he is saying, or Shakespeare is: you must not argue with God's appointed; Coriolanus was right and he was murdered by infamy.

I enjoy Munich. Isolation, peace, tranquillity, and a new world. Walk for miles and drink a perfect cappuccino in the teahouse under a light drizzle. The huge sunshades are folded down and I request one of them up since they must have a double purpose both for sun and rain. I am told by the waitress that this is not possible. They are only for the sun! I know now that I am without doubt in Germany and that no other race on earth would forbid the opening of umbrellas in the rain merely because they are usually used for sunshine. So I have to go inside and sit in the smoky restaurant. I must confess to finding this bizarre and utterly German but since everything else is so perfect, one has to forgive them.

As I leave the park the cafés are just opening up and the plates are piled high with food. The city is very beautiful and I cannot get over the variety and richness of the Kellers with their well-carpentered tables in light wood, perfectly clean and smelling good. Homely food, giant tables, happy and contented people eating and drinking in an atmosphere of peace and tranquillity.

To teatime with the other Günther, who is my dramaturg on *Coriolanus*. He lives with his charming wife, who works for

German TV, and we both share our admiration for Olivier. We discuss his televised *Othello*, which she had bought for German TV. I tend to talk too much and exaggerate an incident, which shows you how isolation can overcharge you. I speak about Olivier's death and how it resulted in me directing my first show at the National Theatre, and I made a kind of sepulchral event out of it, since I was in the office at the theatre exactly on the hour he died. On his death his widow, Joan Plowright, was forced to cancel the production she was about to embark on directed by Nuria Espert, the famous Spanish director. So by this circuitous route I was given a job in death by Laurence Olivier, since a replacement had to be found for the Lorca play that Joan Plowright was acting in and I was handy. Hence, after all this time, I was to do *Salome*.

I had wondered how on earth I was going to achieve the ambition of playing Herod in my own production and sadly saw the chances dwindling away since the Irish company I had directed at the Gate in Dublin were taking their prize everywhere and making it more and more difficult for me to perform it; they eventually took it to the Edinburgh Festival, thus preventing me from doing it in London. But I was still determined, even if my performance was to be compared to the Irish Herod, and do it I would. Olivier seems to have made this possible, since there would have been no other way that the regime would have willingly taken me on or, at least, that was my subjective interpretation of the facts. Since the National seemed to embody the spirit of Olivier it seemed fitting that on the very rare occasion that I had a meeting there, once in years, I should have chosen that precise time, of Olivier's death, and even then it was after my agent made two cancellations.

We talk for a couple of hours and have tea and biscuits. Günther and his wife live in one of those large end-of-century Art Nouveau-designed buildings which have wide corridors as you enter where you could put a desk. We also discuss Shakespeare's text and the words which have slipped out of use and often mean their opposite and might be translated the wrong way. Thus, Coriolanus saying, "What would you have, you curs, that like not peace nor war? The one affrights you, the other makes you proud." I had never really understood proud, unless it meant proud of being in a state of peace, but as any schoolboy now knows, proud then meant boastful, loud, arrogant, and, of course, it makes sense once again. This German professor knows his Shakespeare. He also studies me so as to be primed up when composing his programme notes, reads my books, reviews, newspaper articles.

We talk of the role of director as producer and I have to disagree with his opinion that a director should run a company, since I have noted a caution in directors employing me; while the reverse was felt when I was employed by producers, who sought talent from all areas with no threat to their person or creativity. The producer has no axe to grind nor fears competition since he or she merely seeks out what will fill the theatre. Apart from this, the director is not available for his actors, to hear their griefs or to solve problems, as he is often dealing with problems of his own and has little time to oversee glaring mistakes and indulgences being committed in the early stages of rehearsal where an astute eye might have brought it back from chaos. I have heard of other companies who *never* see their director. Günther Beelitz might err the other way since he sees his actors almost daily as a matter of course, dropping into rehearsals and always being there, unless abroad searching out other directors. His office is always available and our company might have broken down with misunderstandings had he not been there to pour oil over the stormy waters. Joe Papp was the same in New York, always there for the actors who do need to feel that they can refer to some higher figure for comfort in times of stress. Unless you are a single one-play-at-a-time company, to have a director stretched to create and administer is a prescription for disaster and safety.

We discuss the verse and, strangely, Günther comes out in favour of rhyming verse, which the actors tend to resist. I too resist the idea and view verse as being like a form of jazz where you slip in and out of the rhythm and always go for meaning. On the way home I find a most perfect Chinese restaurant in the basement of the Gallery Stück.

Monday 17th June

There is something intensely satisfying about doing a play you have done once before . . . You can conduct it at a pace since it is familiar, re-define, re-examine. I get up early and the rain never ceases, just a constant drizzle. The old lady in the building opposite whose room faces mine has not yet put out the food for the pigeons.

I walk to work in the rain after having discovered a sauna in the basement of the hotel — I lay in the heat fantasising . . . I get to work determined to make the most of the limited time and dive into rehearsal. I choose to start with the Tribunes meeting Menenius and re-do the plotting, keeping to one confined space, reacting to the language in small moves almost as a routine with the two Tribunes bracketing Menenius like bookends. Again the lamb versus the bear image. They meet in the street and we devise all sorts of physical mannerisms. The Tribunes creep around the body of Menenius, fascinated by his power, and try to get close and familiar, but Menenius has no interest in them except as a boss trying to keep in with union leaders so as to avoid a strike.

The scene works well and the atmosphere created by the musician unfolds the play almost with the mood of a film. I work five hours non-stop with no break except for the actors, who go to the canteen, but I forget the poor musician and stage management and now I'm exhausted. Will break tomorrow. We quickly stage the greetings on Coriolanus' return with his mother, doing it as a series of slow figure eights as each member greets the other in turn, hugging, welcoming and then turning to the next one. It works very well, far better than in New York when the cast couldn't be bothered to move in any way but the way they walk to the shopping mall. Here they at least seize the slow motion and it gives the event the heightened feeling of ritual and celebration of the returning warrior. I have to stand up all day to be part of it . . . whenever I sit down I feel passive. The atmosphere is better, clearer and I speak more about the characters and the scene but the play is so long and unfolds relentlessly, scene after scene without stop . . . The chorus of soldiers perform a vocal welcome for Coriolanus, splitting up the syllables into Co-ri-o-la-nus, their voices rising on each repetition until it sounds like an opera in the style of Orff's *Carmina Burana*. It is tremendously exciting and the music comes underneath and swells it. It is so thrilling I make them do it several times.

Rufus seems less like Coriolanus today but soldiers on and gives indications that it is within him but he must winkle it out. The Tribune, Brutus, enjoys growing into his slug-like part as it seems to bring out the worst of his characteristics but he convinces in his seedy menace. Menenius grows more than ever into his role as a stalwart, good-natured and patrician; with his small prescription glasses, with their DDR frames, he is perfect. He never questions what is obvious and has no 'problem'.

After the grand ceremonial greetings for the victor, and

their exit out of the woodwork, come the two Tribunes, apparently speaking for the people; in Shakespeare's text they seem to be more like Marxist revolutionaries who wish to depose their master's economic repression but who nevertheless keep the country in order and safe. Shakespeare appears to endorse Coriolanus' view or gives him the stance of one who not only hates the democratic ideal but believes that when you give in to majority taste you are doomed since you embrace the taste of the illiterate masses. The masses desire simple lives and peace while the Führers desire conquests and gains and need the masses for their bodies and labour. The Generals and Senators take pride in their conquests and they love nothing more than to show their 'scars' to the people and each scar is a victory for Volumnia like academy awards in the flesh.

Volumnia greets Menenius before the celebration with utter joy and delights in the twenty-five wounds that Coriolanus has suffered, adoring her killer boy for each cut as if it were her. He bleeds for Mum and she revels in it. The oedipal son. It is as if her female body has inherited a passivity that she hates and her spirit seeks redress by making her son her surrogate self. So he strikes out for his Mum, like a Frankenstein's monster that she helped to create, as all good sons do whose mother is the source of their pride rather than a father who gives a man his initiation into the world. The mother may give her hatred of men onto the son. She revels like a she-wolf . . . "Top of the world, Ma", shrieks Cagney as he goes to his dramatic, fiery apotheosis and confirms the oedipal link. The Kray twins, those masterminders of East End villainy, confirmed their adoration for Ma Violet in many a gesture of compliance but at the same time they had a pride in being the claws of Ma. Weak female Ma who influences the tiger and makes the beast a female-male. A very dangerous species.

Not for Dad, who already is an image of strength and needs no protecting, but for the vulnerable soft-dugged Ma, wrapping you up with kisses and fluffing pillows. Nobody hurts Ma, OK? And also this means nobody touches you since Ma loves you, and in fact is in you; if you are hurt, attacked or criticised then Ma is hurt, and no-one is allowed to do that. Mother is introjected into the male body is obviously what I am saying. So although the villain/gangster is a mini-Mum he has all the strength of the male. Eureka! He can avenge his mother's hurts all his life. The mother/son naturally can do no wrong and in killing the father he merely destroys mother's enemy. After all, the son is related by blood, whereas the father will never be related to Mum. Who has not at some time wanted to kill his Dad? The outside critical impartial world becomes 'Dad' . . . You must take on the world and must be accepted or worshipped like Ma is. Only worship is enough to pay the interest for the young female spirit who may have been abused all her life, but now she's inside him like a demon. Controlled, this female demon can make you a fierce warrior, achiever, or a good soldier or helper, but uncontrolled you could be a Hitler, a Dali, a Sylvester Stallone.

We reach deep into the play and arrive at the meeting of the senate, whereby Coriolanus is appointed 'Counsel', albeit reluctantly, he claims, since he'd rather be the people's 'servant' than sway with them. We stage the proceedings in a circle of chairs representing a board meeting while Cominius needlessly regurgitates the fabulous exploits in a rodomontade whose kindest act would be to cut it severely, which we do. Perhaps Shakespeare wanted to give a friend a few more lines, since Cominius has not too much to do and needs a persuasive speech to convince the members of the senate. It's very evident what Coriolanus has achieved, since it's mentioned when he comes bleeding from the battle and again when he re-enters Rome, but in case the audience have come in late it's about to be 'repeated' for those who missed the first two episodes. Anyone entering now would be able, from this speech, to enjoy the play as if it had just begun. Cominius encapsulates everything that has happened until now. Many of Shakespeare's plays seem to be written with a built-in refresher speech, as if audiences were in the habit of entering late or when they wished, or to see a special player, and so it is possible that he wrote with this in view. In *Hamlet* you could easily enter after the first long scene which sets up the plot with the ghost, but you won't miss it if you come in a scene later since it is repeated by the King.

The conclusion of the meeting is that Coriolanus must now appeal to the people with the ritualistic exposure of his wounds so that they may 'see' his sacrifices on their behalf. Interestingly enough it occurs to me at last what stripes and medals symbolise, since these are now worn outside to describe the wounds on the inside.

It is still raining today and I go downtown into the grey drizzle to buy some notebooks and am again enchanted by Munich. The city. I find a stationer's shop that has everything in the world in it. Notebooks of every size and description . . . leather-bound notebooks and hand-bound notebooks . . . row upon row of every bizarre piece of office gallimaufry you could imagine. Stack upon stack of junk to pollute the bursting ash can of the world. Once a typewriter had just a ribbon but now they have different ribbons set in plastic containers that have to be jettisoned mid-sentence and you find you have run out so you buy half a dozen at a time; once you typed for a day with a mere shade lighter impact from the ribbon.

Then, feeling hungry from my tortuous investigations of the

vagaries of bureaucracy, I head for the simpler delights of nosh. I have not eaten all day and so go to the large market square, which seems to house the entire food and tastes of Munich. The square is a collection of small huts or cafés, each with its own specialities and clientele. It is utterly gemütlich. The faces are content as each have found their own favourite and I now have to find mine. One place sells meat, another bread, bratwurst, and every variety of flesh the human mind is capable of conceiving. The fish shop has small round tables to sample the wares and seems to possess every single thing that lives in sea or river. The delicatessen has varieties of salads beyond belief — an endless array of colours and tastes. People sit contentedly at small tables. I love tradition if it means holding on to the best of the past and refining it through the decades. Holding what is valuable and meaningful to your life rather than ripping it out like tired veins.

I have an obsession to eat a plain Vienna hotdog with mustard, but that is too simple for this market square. I gaze in awe as one from another planet, and even from the relative abundance of Britain I cannot believe the sheer multitude, not greed, not gargantuan displays but just great imagination and variety. I flash back to the grim Tobacco Wharf and to my refurbished warehouse, beautifully restored, in the East End docks. It is like a morgue and not one food shop exists and you are forced to walk past an endless display of boutiques. Here each shop has a small table at which you could eat and, of course, it is a food market, so I cannot compare it to the ghastly sterile Tobacco Wharf, except that the wharf might have made an effort to draw people with at least a couple of food emporiums, but the sad fact is that the Brits are both lazy and not terribly imaginative in that department.

Tuesday 18th June

The play is still buzzing round my head. Can't get the mood right in the 'voices' scene . . . the citizens are too clownish. Watch out for that or it might end up looking two-dimensional.

It has finally stopped raining after two days. I walk in and out of the Kellers, each one like a huge barn big enough to take a battalion. The cleanliness is legendary . . . a large wooden table to make you feel you're in your own kitchen where you are safe . . . cosy, friendly, warm and smelling good. Candles on tables. A solo person can feel OK and even good bathing in his own thoughts amidst a tranquil sanctuary. The gemütlich Bavarian menu with its emphasis on meat, the never-ending animals served in every different shape, taste, size, colour, stewed, cold, hot, steamed, roasted, pickled, boiled, charcoaled, cured, and tumbling down the counter endless sausages like logs falling, cascading and piled on to large white plates with mountains of sauerkraut and potatoes . . . and the small tables in the food store where you taste, nibble, stuff, gorge, feast with your eyes . . .

I start rehearsal today with a part of my mind elsewhere, a small part invaded by another world outside *Coriolanus*. A life that exists beyond these grey walls and the German language squeezing out Shakespeare but you cannot allow a smidgen to invade your brain. When directing your mind must be an open room which has been stripped bare to the essentials and which you choose to decorate as you will. Your life is recreated on that stage or in that room and if there is something else in the room it will continually clash. You must extirpate it. Get rid of it!

When I did the play in New York I was unleashed and free

and terrified but excited by the new. A play I had no experience of, and all my wits were on full alert and the room was cleared out. I lived in the Grammercy Park Hotel and had breakfast each morning in the diner on Third Avenue and 21st Street, after a jog round the square. I walked to work at the Public Theater in Lafayette down in the Village past all the homeless and jobless selling junk in an area just in front of the theatre. With a big sigh of apprehension I steamed in. I had no knowledge of the play and it was forged in the furnace I kept fired in my mind. My concentration was immense since my life depended on it. Joe Papp came in from time to time and seemed satisfied with the progress. His Shakespeare marathon was more goodwill than good work and he desperately needed a good one. So he came in to check it out and liked what he saw and I was determined to do a good job for Joe, for me and for *Coriolanus*. I was thus inspired and took it to heart, heated my mind in fire and brimstone and concentrated with a will that allowed no distractions in the room. I even remember finding my ubiquitous camera too much in my bag and so I left that at the hotel. No distraction, but a monklike devotion to the task, but then when I came out at night into the warm but going-to-wintry New York it was dark and the atmosphere was electric. I was so happy to leave the theatre where I had stayed for the five or six hours. I wouldn't leave the rehearsal room for a moment and I am sure there must be many directors who work like this. The bracing air and smell of New York would hit me like perfume and there was a nifty Mexican cantina across the way, which did you a famous margarita, or I would meet my ex-wife, Shelley Lee, and we'd tumble into a sushi bar. But the feeling after rehearsals like that were as of a purgation of the spirit. Now in Munich, reproducing what I discovered is not the same feeling and it doesn't work with different ingredients in the same way and so subtle adjustments have to be made. Rufus Beck is not

Christopher Walken with his gangster shtick but it still works for Rufus as the hunted wolf. Politics, history and culture make great play about how different human beings are in different countries and how irreconcilable are our differences, and yet when you direct actors you find that the differences are not so great beneath the surface at all. In fact, strip the layer of conditioning off, which is one thin onion skin, and people are the same the world over and in acting you are always going just that much beneath the surface of civilised behaviour or you would be too inhibited to do it. The actors respond to the same stimuli, laugh at the same gags, and are moulded by the same situations. Each actor has the same problem with a line as his counterpart in New York. Only before or after rehearsal, when the veneer is put back, does one see the differences, when the protective coating of the national culture is applied. So the play moves ahead like a juggernaut.

We begin by recalling the entrance of Coriolanus to Rome and Volumnia comes in and welcomes him as the cast begin their slow figures of eight, clasping, smiling, reacting with delight. Now they link hands and give the impression, as they step forward, of royalty facing a huge crowd, as they smile and wave from the steps of the senate. They bow to the imaginary mob and say their lines with the smile for the audience and their words for their colleagues, the way actors do at a curtain call, smiling hypocritically, while under their breath voicing their true thoughts. Bending in supplication they are apt to say, "Lousy audience tonight. . ." Since becoming what is laughingly called an actor-manager, I hate this, because those eggs out there are my guests and have voted for me with their feet and their loose change . . . Mum swells with pride and predicts the 'presidency' for her son . . . "There's one thing wanting, which I doubt not but our Rome will cast upon thee

. . ." Coriolanus resists but is coerced by her pride to take the steps that will lead to his demise. The next step he must take is to win the hearts of the people with a strange ceremony of acting, like a Hyde Park orator, and seeking the 'voices' or the votes of the people. It is the ceremony that all politicians adore, begging for the hearts of the people whom they will eventually betray once in power.

The citizens turn up and decide to give him a hearing. Menenius arrives with a short ladder under his arm that Coriolanus will use, one of those free-standing affairs shaped in an inverted 'V'. Frankly, I felt it was a poorly written scene and very difficult to stage without sounding monotonous and making the citizens seem obtuse. The set-up is too obvious. Our musician creates a kind of 'yokel' music, a rhythmic 'dum-ti-dum' that suits them admirably. They willingly accept Coriolanus, awed perhaps by the presence of the great man in his humble weeds. The citizens circle him, react to his double-entendres, provoke a few limited responses from him, while he exercises admirable restraint.

I decide to bring all the citizens on at once rather than in pairs, since it looks like advancing crowds of geeks let out for the day. The combined simple-mindedness amplifies all the more their fawning helplessness in front of the aristocrat and they stare at and applaud the Hyde Park orator. But they wish to see his wounds and he must perforce, as part of the ceremony, reveal them and show that he is a man of the people who got his wounds defending them so in exchange they must give him their voices. But Coriolanus can't find the heart to stoop to such a debasing act and avoids having to do it by some fancy verbals. The scene has one good speech in it for Coriolanus, when he dismisses antiquated custom. The scene was always a problem until the end, but we create a sense of atmosphere and 'speakers' corner' familiarity.

Since yesterday I worked for five hours without a break and was shattered after, I decide today to go to the canteen for twenty minutes. The workers and actors are taking away plates piled high with mashed and stewed concoctions, separated into different departments or dividers on the plate itself, so as to keep the salad pristine. I decide to sit with Karlheinz and so I grab a soup and I join him. Karlheinz, who plays the minor part of Titus Lartius, tells me his foot is in agony from a stage fall he took last year and he wants me to spare him from the production. He has private treatment. I ask him about German medical care and explain that in the UK it is largely free under the Health Service. He thinks that the lazy would exploit this. The 'idle ones' as he colourfully christens them. I have noticed in my travels outside the UK that many nations' citizens think, or rather hold a firm belief, that the idle ones must not be looked after for free. An American girl, who was staying with her businessman father at my hotel, voiced similar anxieties about the poor or 'idle'. When I told her about working in New York her swift-as-a-fart response was that they should deport a lot of the unemployed who didn't *want* to work. She persisted that if they really wanted to work they should be happy to do house-cleaning. Being so repellent in her ideas made my gorge rise but I tried to swallow down the bile that her nasty self-satisfied opinions pulled from my throat. Apparently they found getting a 'cleaner' more difficult than they expected with all the cheap labour around. She was thick as pig-shit and knew nothing about the culture of New York nor, of course, had she ever heard of Shakespeare's *Coriolanus*. She thought of herself as pretty and she is happy to be in Munich to do some 'shopping'. Her father was there pushing his medical products.

I leave Karlheinz in his happy opinions, which seem to have a little redolence of some not-too-distant past, and can see that in the nineties to talk about the 'idle' in this way makes you a surefire candidate for the Adolf 2 Party. I go sullenly back to rehearsal and we do the aftermath of the last scene where the citizens are being abused by the two union leaders or Tribunes for having given their voices so easily and to recant. We turn it into a kind of Keystone Cops scene, with the citizens rushing off to reverse the decisions and screeching to a halt as the Tribunes remember one more instruction for them and then rushing off and repeating the action of start-stop. Hence the many-headed multitude who run this way and that with the tide, heads like seaweed waving in the ebbing waters. I haven't really burned up any inspiration today but at 4pm we are ready to split. So we leave and the sun comes out and I wonder what to do for the next nineteen hours until 11am the next day. I wander into a high-priced deli-cum-café called the Kafer which is famous for its restaurant bar. I descend the stairs of this opulent emporium where all the foods of the earth tumble out of their baskets in profusion. To the right of the meat counter is tucked away this charming little restaurant with a few tables and stools at the bar. It feels almost too opulent for me to be in and I always have this sneaking suspicion that they will detect my unfamiliarity with opulence and will show me the door, but they don't and I am seated. Everyone is intensely German upper-class with that kind of sneery, thin-lipped look and cold blue eyes. To be even a Jew in such a place feels uncomfortable if not unsafe. All bright expensive faces nosing their select cuisine and, of course, nearly all smoking as if the word cancer had never been invented. I enjoy a herring in apple sauce with such choice rolls from a basket. With my herring I read *Life* magazine, which is full of high-definition colour pictures of dying Kurds freezing to death amidst advertisements for Las Vegas resorts and autos.

I leave and the sun is still out. My loneliness out here is like an acid wearing me down to the bone. A friend I am supposed to see has cancelled . . . Back in my hotel I lie on my big spongy bed and roll over as if to escape in sleep, but then decide to take a long walk. The little cafés near the park and the Bierstubes are full of happy chatting people. All the cafés are full, especially the small cute one in the corner of the park. They look so enchanting and inviting, lit in golden amber glows and I long to go in for the warmth of their company, but a lone person is a handicapped one in some places. I walk off the feeling and get into a sweat and then I wander into my next-door café-pub. There are no pubs here as such, where you only booze. Food here goes hand in hand with drink and all the pubs serve good tasty dinners at night. My next-door Gasthaus is like a painting . . . a group of nine men sit under two wicker lamps and could have been painted by an early Van Gogh. It is a simple place and I am quite happy to be alone here. Four booths are occupied by other single folk whose only companion is their dinner. I order a Frankenwein as a treat and a spaghetti bolognese and take out my notebook. I order a second quarter of the tasty white wine, an '88 Volkacher Kirchberg. Very nice! It's like a sanctuary in here in this cheap local where the neighbourhood go each night. Men play cards at the next table, tossing unwanted cards into the centre and playing for money. At the end of the room the table of nine has depleted its number. The smoke curls into the wicker lamp. A young couple have just arrived for their evening meal and are studying the menu. There is a painting on the wall which looks like this pub and it's dated 1878. The ceiling is dark brown aided by years of stale fag smoke and the TV is permanently off. Probably Nazis in uniform sat in here.

Wednesday 19th June

Slept fitfully, woke and it was still dark outside, fell back asleep and woke at 6.13 and waited until 6.30 to order breakfast. We are one hour ahead of Britain and so while Britain snoozes . . . but everything seems to stay open later too. My breakfast arrives — muesli, orange juice and rolls — and the chambermaid always puts something extra on my tray in a kind of motherly way and so this morning I am treated to a whole plate of cold meats and cheese, and a boiled egg, which I can't eat. I am aware that somewhere someone is starving while I glumly reject all this food. I walk to the theatre and have a coffee in the canteen. It's nearly twelve and so I treat myself to another snack. The workers are gathering their multi-divided piled-up plates. On the walls are sentimental pictures of clowns and a photo of the staff football team. A couple of fruit machines are at the far end. In the kitchen a Bavarian granny is rolling the mix for the dumplings and I tentatively request my favourite which is the German frankfurter, mysteriously unavailable elsewhere; she plucks one out of a bowl of hot water and, armed with a roll, I contentedly take my booty to the table. I am still bothered about the 'voting' scene — the voices. It doesn't work and we must look at it again because I always expect that if I concentrate hard it will suddenly appear like magic, since everything has so far. I am peeved that this scene hasn't and I will search for it. A staff worker has just sat down with four Viennas. My one is suddenly not enough and I reckon I could now eat six.

In my hotel room this morning I felt like Joseph K in *The Trial*, haunted in his room by the presence of a female next door. He needs to talk to her. Germany is very Kafkaesque and Kafka's lonely eye perfectly captures the details of a white blouse hanging on the window which Joseph K observes while he's being arrested. From my room my lonely eye rests and captures details opposite. I see an old lady who daily feeds the pigeons. I admire the interlapping roof tiles, so perfectly aligned with never a tile loose.

Thursday 20th June

The breakfast room in this four-star hotel is filling up with the ghastly business types who make up society in any city, awful money-hardened faces and expressions. Their ugly, brutal-looking wives staring like junkies at the breakfast buffet, their mis-shapen figures barely masked by the hideous clothes they wear to recontour themselves. The inevitable cig stuck out of their mouths or burning relentlessly in their fingers, and the awful coughs. The waitress is a thick-waisted Bavarian with the cruellest face I have ever seen on a young woman. It is a face devoid of a shred of human feeling, a lumpy porridgy waxen orb, and it convinces me that the death camp warders who were women were best drawn from Bavaria, with their stolid expressionless demeanour walking around with the whips. Last week there was a march of 2,000 Nazis in Dresden in honour of the Nazi Rainer Sontag, who was shot and killed. That the march was allowed to air the grievances of these potential murderers is amazing.

The larger waitress seems to have taken a shine to me and dollops on extras every day now. This morning she wears a red ribbon in her hair atop her porcine but attractive face.

So back to *Coriolanus*. We re-do the voices and if one person gives off that special energy it seems to light up the others. The group are a pleasant bunch but Thomas, an older man in his fifties, has a clear cutting edge that defines him. He penetrates the air with a sharp succinct tone. The voters have now become a crowd of hecklers, brave in mass but when Coriolanus picks on one and the spotlight is on an individual, the heckler shrinks. Coriolanus clicks his fingers to bid the heckler come over. The poor citizen loses his power of anonymity and is placed on the spot, and it works. Martin the musician still introduces them as a bunch of golems. We have made a breakthrough and it is now very funny. We see them being won over by Coriolanus, and they are concerned, thoughtful, murmuring and acquiescent. Coriolanus leaves, having won the primaries and in good nick to win the presidency. The two Tribunes come on and are welcomed by the soporific, grinning-like-idiot faces of the mob, who think they have acquitted themselves well. The crowd is not responding in unison to the questions as if still stoned by the presence of their hero. The Tribunes are furious and believe the people were fooled by platitudes, which they were, for Shakespeare had penned a rather thinnish speech of persuasion with no words of corn, rights, respect, but only a blathering desire to be counsel and he didn't even reveal his wounds! Coriolanus says coyly: "I have wounds to show you, which shall be yours in private." Not in public at all — or is this a naughty line to some appealing lusty worker?

So again the plebs are harassed, bullied, reprimanded by their spokesmen and off they run again, trying to undo the deed, the many-headed multitude, whose brains run ". . . north, south, east and west". The Tribunes give them their instructions and we again play the game of false exits. Now along come the gang of four: Coriolanus, Menenius, Cominius and Titus (missing, bad leg, so we give his lines to Cominius). So the gang of three are taking a walk to the marketplace for confirmation of their votes. Chris Walken in New York devised a kind of bully-boy strut, which is reminiscent of the tough guys' walk in the London suburb of Stamford Hill many years ago, a kind of lurch from right to left with the arms bent and the hands or fists near the chest. The music, naturally from this gifted composer-player, gets right inside the skin. The stroll allows us to take our time over the journey, since the impression is given of walking, although the movement is from side to side, very little space is taken between steps and they are almost walking on the spot. From the other side the two Tribunes appear. Here the scene is played in profile, with the two coming from one side and the gang of three approaching from the other until they become like two groups of raging dogs, pulling against their master's leash. This demands some choreography of when to move forward in order to pull away. They rage at a distance, make feints, shrug in contempt, attack, become furious, maddened, cold, murderous, all within a short period of time. We keep it working and it starts to come to life as Coriolanus becomes the rottweiler, growing incensed and yet held back by the restraining gestures and hands of his two colleagues who step in front of him, much the same way as two street fighters being controlled by mates.

On the dot of 4pm one of the actors, in keeping with his union status in the character of the Tribune, says he has to go . . . he has a performance at 8pm. He has done little hard work all day, since we started with the voters' scene, but he has to go and it's as if a giant electric band has released me and I am free.

A friend of a chum in LA is in town, one of those film people who make deals and are involved in that endless movie babble and yack that goes on forever, like some kind of Beckettian script on acid. Their talk is so complex and dead that it leads eventually to a kind of cirrhosis of the soul just being in their company for one hour. Creativity seems to be only the merest thin gruel that provides an outlet for their madness and globe-trotting. I know the creative act and that's all I wish to know. In the theatre I know a little more as one would, since it is necessary to buy a ticket and that must cover the costs of the rent and the actors and if it doesn't, too bad. The backers get 60% of the profits and end of message. On film the shenanigans are prostitution of ethics, the lying and inveigling, the snobbism, the dealing, the foreign rights, the above-the-line and below-the-line, the banks, the gormless young producers in Armani suits that slither around Cannes with their dreary spouses, the desperation of other producers to meet the 'money men', the knee-jerking towards stars whose ability is less than any good stage actor in sheer pound for pound drive, ability or skill and yet are made into icons because their performance is multiplied on a thousand screens and belief in their own omnipotence, the slobbering around these film jerks whose every fart is held up for scrutiny as if they were words from Plato and so it is not with relish that I talk to these creatures, or the people who pursue them or their loathsome parties where each small name wishes to brush near a bigger name and where the women desperately try to trade whatever they have for a smell of glory. This affects me in some way, as my work is often touted to these anonymous multi-tentacled groups.

We meet and his conversation bores me as rigidly as I thought it would . . . His friend, who is a video buyer, turns up and tells me how instinctive he is in getting his work together, and how he is a partner with a giant Yankee corporation and more blather and bullshit. I don't know what they are talking about but I try to establish a bridge across this sea of boredom. I start as usual to feel inferior without an office and a few secretaries and deals coming out of my arse. Not being involved directly in the art of doing but very importantly in what they do leaves me feeling empty and squalid.

I recognise that not only do we need these people, but they also create work by their need to get things made for screens, video and silver all over the world. However, I am left in a kind of daze. I don't like their way of life nor their faces . . . I remember Cannes and all the smug, dozy cretins swimming around like germs ready to fasten themselves onto anything that might yield them something . . . too much here, I do protest too much . . . but even my loneliness is somehow sweeter than this and I long for the daydreams of isolation and my notebook. I know that good producers are worth their weight in gold and can bring together by their taste the best elements, but most follow the same worn-out routine as they do in the UK, hence the death of the film industry and when one looks at the jerks running it one is not surprised.

So we sit and I listen to the high-pitched falsettto of my LA friend. The bum didn't see *The Trial* even if it was on for several months at the National and this same man represents my interests and tries to sell my works. He also means well and tries his hardest to sell the screen rights of my play *Kvetch* (just won the *Evening Standard* Best Comedy award) but he missed it on stage, naturally. He then, 'jokingly', asks this German producer we are having this by now tasteless dinner with if he would cough up a few bob as if I was a product in a suitcase and if you don't like this one, try this. He now appears like a cheap door-to-door salesman and is embarrassing me. They are all salesmen and I *hate* salesmen, having been one for a number of dead years in the distant past.

First they take us to this kind of restaurant full of young trendy things and since I was in Bavaria I wanted a Bierkeller with giant wooden tables and fat Bavarians stuffing themselves with Leberwurst. Instead we are crowded into this yuppie nursery, which they obviously feel at home in, the kind of carzey seen on every street corner in West Hollywood. Then we shift to a Russian restaurant, with more young toddlers, who sit by candlelight and our German friend, Rainer, who is very nice to me, is singing the praises of an American director who is the current 'hot' in the USA. There is one thing I detest in my presence and that is the eulogising of someone else's art, implying that the present company are less endowed and are overawed by the work of some minor 'artiste'. Praise is OK but this fawning I find intolerable, since artists are a bit like women in temperament and you don't talk about how lovely a woman is in front of another woman. The current 'hot' director is Peter Sellars and the current 'hot' choreographer is Mark Morris, whose work I much admired in Brussels when I went to see Baryshnikov there to discuss his playing in my production of *Metamorphosis*, so I feel forced to throw in my threepence-worth of crapology. So I suggest we repair to some famous Keller which, with due respect to their sensibilities, must seem like a low-class pub to them. Here we are met by another two people, since these types are terribly gregarious and are somehow never happy unless there are too many people at the table and the waiters have to find more chairs and nobody can sit comfortably and you never really speak to anybody, since there are always eight people rabbiting at the same time.

I order Leberwurst and a giant tankard of beer. The pale things that arrive look like what a sick dog might have shat out and so I pass them around. I eat some soggy potatoes and overcooked sauerkraut. My friend George from LA is in good spirits and keeps screeching and then my early warning detector, my ulcer, starts to bite me, screaming to get out. The video producer then says some things which in my present situation seem opportunistic, that the best thing lovers can give each other is freedom and that is the greatest form of love between two people. Sounds also like a recipe for having your cake and eating it. What in 'Yankee nursery babble' is called cheating. I am eventually glad to escape to bed with a glass of milk for my hurt stomach.

Friday 21st June

Back into what is now my regular haunt, the Kafer café, the small secret basement which I am getting to like, even if everyone here looks like a pure Aryan. All the women are pinched, tight, blonde and shoulder-padded and sit at the bar gaily blowing their ubiquitous fags over the counter. I could have landed in the inner sanctum of the Nazi elite. I could also be making a horrendous error. A tall, silver-haired Curt Jurgens type strolls over with his blonde. It's a minute Fortnum and Mason and there are some plump little brown-eyed children who look pale with lack of exercise, who are struggling to eat dishes that cost £7 or £8 each. The two smokers at the bar have lit two more cigs.

At rehearsal today Rufus absents himself with a cold and loss of voice though he could, I thought, have plotted some work without using his voice. However, in Germany they announce their absences with no court of appeal. We work well without him and conclude the scene when the citizens rush on to help the Tribunes, who are being manhandled by Coriolanus. The sweep of bodies rushing across the stage is exciting and powerful, again the power is in the sudden freeze at the end of the run as if the collected energy of the effort has been impacted into the still position. It is brute power and suggests people of great anger but contained and deadly . . . So they rush on, freeze to block Coriolanus and release the Tribunes. A further group covers the flank with another small burst . . . Coriolanus and his gang are trapped . . . The next move is where the citizens rush Coriolanus and the groups exchange positions as if weaving through each other . . . They now face each other from opposite sides of the stage . . . Once more the cry of "Seize them" . . . The mob charge and this time Coriolanus and the senators escape the flight of bodies by side-stepping on to the rostrum . . . The crowd now are facing upstage and Coriolanus facing down and slightly higher than them and so we see a mass of angry, twisted backs facing Menenius, Coriolanus and Cominius. Menenius pleads for peace and calm but the many-headed multitude have no individuality except at the lowest level of mob hysteria. They are one mass, linked and multiplied by the energy their mass represents. Coriolanus is trapped and in the bravura of the moment confronts them: "No, I'll die here. There's some among you have beheld me fighting: come, try upon yourselves what you have seen me."

Coriolanus proceeds to draw his sword but in our modern version we have no weapons as such. He merely walks steadily and calmly to one of the Tribunes and delivers a pile-driver — whack! — that starts the melee. We organise the kind of punch-up seen in wild west saloons to the rhythm of a drum. We choreograph a fist-fight with two blows delivered to a man, which is reciprocated, and it works in that kind of precision and the actors really relish doing it. We organise a fairly complete battle in half an hour by establishing the rules of the blows. As one man mimes striking the other and the drum marks the blow, the recipient of the blow staggers, recovers and then strikes back and so the process is repeated and it's very effective and at the same time very funny. Eventually the mob are beaten off and as they stagger from the stage the three

John Waynes rub their knuckles gingerly. They are well satisfied and Coriolanus boasts: "On fair ground I could beat forty of them", while Menenius, puffing, adds his two cents' worth: "I could myself take up a brace o' the best of them . . ." The scene is funny, expresses the confusion and suddenness of violence, is a fight and yet is a demonstration of one and makes the movie reference which immediately makes an impact on the filing system in the audience's head.

Again one of the actors who plays the Tribune wears the demeanour of sour complaint when the scene has worked so well, and his grey German face with its sagging whine brings us down. The young actor playing the Herald is even forced to admonish him and say: "Das ist nicht so schlimm [it's not so bad]". In other words, belt up. The day then proceeds without Coriolanus and we even dip into Act Two. We finish early but have moved across the planet *Coriolanus* like a bunch of devouring locusts chewing up everything in sight.

Saturday 22nd June

Bad sleep, terrible stomach pains relating to emotional entrapment. Sona comes to watch the rehearsal since she seems fascinated in the process. As I said, I don't generally like viewers because they induce a certain self-consciousness if they are not directly in rehearsal. We repeat the happy citizens' scene a few times, when we witness their apparent pleasure at Coriolanus' exile, really for lack of anything else to do as so many are absent, and I split.

Sona meets me later for a drink. She was brought up in the

USA and came to Germany just twelve years ago. She certainly wouldn't do much acting in Punkville, USA, but in Germany she can play Shakespeare and Schiller as routine theatre fare and sing in her concerts of Brecht/ Weill. She is an animated sculptured-faced lady with a broad jawline and vivid blue eyes that are forever alive with concern, ideas, thoughts and emotions . . . nothing deadly here. She has a look of an Egon Schiele portrait and I know she is very respectful of my work and when she came over to see *The Trial* she saw both matinée and evening performances and admired it greatly, which naturally pleased me all the more, since I would be working with her and I knew she would spread the word among the suspicious German actors, one of whom we have mentioned and who will be destined to figure in my fate in the future. After this particular sour-faced actor had left the room I stood on my little soapbox and declared that in twenty years of directing I had never witnessed such laziness and clock-watching as I have in the German theatre. My stage manager with her perfect English agrees with me completely and suggests that the actors are spoiled and lazy here and work less since the repertoire is larger. She has worked in England and felt the actors worked much harder and were much 'hungrier' and had far more range, but at the same time she found the British theatre extremely pedestrian and slavishly followed the laws of naturalism and were most unadventurous. She added that at the major theatres new forms of theatre were not overly encouraged; of course, things have changed slightly since then and Richard Eyre had me and Complicité in one season and now Robert Lepage and so the light is beginning to dawn in England. However, the stage manager put me thoroughly and politely in my place and with good authority and I had to agree with her. We are separate continents, our two land masses, and yet reading about theatre in Wilde's time over a hundred years ago, there was quite a traffic of French theatre over to London.

Tuesday 25th June

Back in Munich, having taken Monday off! Couldn't get the early plane back after a late night seeing Julia Migenes sing Tosca at Earls Court and having dinner with her and Peter Medak after. I wanted Julia to play Salome in my production of Wilde's play but couldn't get any slob producer to be interested in what could have been enthralling and the most exciting thing of the season. The opera was astounding in the huge Earls Court arena and became, by virtue of the gigantic space, epic theatre, with long running entrances, horses and soldiers, and they staged the whole thing in three weeks, and here, because I took one day off, the cast was 'angry' and reported me to the Führer.

I have to take these weekend breaks since I can be back in an hour and some from Munich to London and quite frankly I get tired of walking the streets and even the luscious English Garden can lose its appeal after too many hours on your tod. They actually rang Günther, who was in Berlin on business, and he had to be involved in their moral turpitude and whining gutlessness. In fact we were so far ahead of the game and had plotted so much I had asked the stage manager to take them through it until I arrived since there was so much that needed repetition — the text alone for memory, the movement and choreography, the battle scenes and slow motion . . . so much opportunity to work out but instead they allowed themselves to fester and destroy something which was working too well, and that was the seat of the problem.

One pale-eyed bastard with all the characteristics of his Hitlerian predecessors, i.e. whining, complaining and most of all informing and destroying, was stirring up the group. The two Tribunes are in themselves perfect Nazis since they are not only underhand but also are narrow in their intentions and mealy-mouthed, hating what is different and wanting power for themselves under the guise of loving the people whom they would eventually lead to destruction. Not for nothing do I have them walking around like sneaky rats, darting, looking left and right before they dare walk. I still could not believe that they could not have worked with a rehearsal director merely for the repetition, as they often do in dance and opera, but then one of these vipers wouldn't have had a chance to complain and whinge.

I have to repeat that at this stage they are, as a group, some of the most complaining, negative actors I have ever worked with. I recall the sheer loving enthusiasm of my Yankee actors, black and white, and this bunch pales into insignificance. It will be that the group will improve once the rotten elements have been weeded out and it may be that the rot infects the others. The sad fact is that I have in two weeks plotted and detailed probably three times as much as any other director would have done and it is sounding and looking very good but perhaps this, in some perverse way, is what is wrong. They want 'Mein Kampf' — to struggle . . .

I ran round my local park in London this morning and felt better for it . . . cut off all softness and in order to brace myself for the task ahead even threw away a romantic poem. Cancelled buying a new property, which was to be a rehearsal space/office/studio/gallery/guest house, but perhaps it is not lost. I can't buy anything when I am working, lest the guilt of joy blunts inspiration. I must be hungry for it and then deflect that hunger into my work.

So I enter the theatre now with a will to commit murder. I see one of the actors who, before I have even opened the door to the rehearsal room, is already whining in glee that Rufus will be away for a week with his cold and what shall we do — "time is running out" his ratty little face whines. I see myself sitting in Brighton and serenely getting on with my autobiography. I see tranquillity and calm — perhaps this is a gift from God. However, the little rumour-monger is wrong, because when I enter the room a sniffly but physically present Rufus is waiting, still muttering about how awful the text is but at least willing to come in while he is 'ill'. He does seem to have an itsy bit of fever but his voice is strong.

We decide to kick off from the beginning to give the chorus a warm-up. Günther enters the room and is about to go when I motion him to stay for a few minutes, since I am proud of this work and would not only not mind some feedback but wish him to see how far we have progressed. Nobody except the lovely Sona MacDonald, and Birgitta, and perhaps the East German actors (two) say anything that's not a complaint. The women love to work and the East Germans don't seem to have the same accessibility to hurt. The others have no word to pass to me of enthusiasm or joy in what they do even though when I watch them I can see them palpably enjoying it.

I go through my straight five hours and then go home without the slightest feedback except from Sona, who will say how good it is looking or how exciting it is to see it grow, or the battle scenes are good . . . So without a little enthusiasm all you seem to have is a bunch of androids who will do as you wish but give no response to you, and that can be a bit painful day after day. So Günther comes in and I feel like a child wanting 'Daddy' to see the work and be excited by it. As Günther watches he mistakenly goes up to the bum informer playing the Tribune, who once again seems to be getting his National Front hackles up. I am watching and talking to the stage manager but I can see what is going on out of the corner of my eye, and that is the whiner pointing in my direction — I believe that is what gets to me, since the fool thinks as I don't speak German I won't interpret his gestures, but body language is one thing I hear loud. There he is, whining, complaining and clouding the air with his foul little eruption. Now the very fact that the scenes he is in work — and are in fact some of the most efficient — seems to be of no consequence to a moron bent on destruction, yet for whatever reason, and let some of those reasons be imagined, he really wants to get filthy. The truth of the matter is that the way I have staged the movement of their scene makes them look twice the players they really are. Even the rest of the cast sit and laugh and relish the scenes. He whines still with Günther, who should be telling him to put up or shut up; his expression, grey, miserable and twisted in malice, has the horrors of everything my imagination feared it would find in Germany.

Today in Germany it is different, and could not be more so, but sometimes my prejudice alights on that cold-blooded blue eye and is rekindled, and what this worm is doing to me now I could very easily see him doing in the bureaucracy of fifty years ago. The same mindless obsession with the outsider who is doing something to him! The man is dangerous. I walk over to his dull, gesticulating figure, that is blasting out to the over-benign Günther his complaining flak of shit. I have to do something since it has reached into my craw and then redoubled, for the play was going very well and everybody was beginning to get into the essence of it. I stand there and tell him calmly that if he is unhappy then he should leave. He looks at first sheepish and then malevolent since the arsehole feels that he is indispensable and nobody gets sacked in Germany. Most of what he says is garbled and untrue — lies that "we're all confused" or "unhappy", which is a crock of shit. I say, "Get out", since I have had enough of his whining. "You are bad for this company," I add, "and we don't need you, you are corrupt" — in the sense that he was corrupting all around him. "I'm corrupt?" he spits pathetically, this whining dog turd, as if all the hours, the sweat, the care, the worry and the loneliness were a sure sign of corruption and not his bleating that he had to go on the dot of 4pm. I don't want any more of this banter with this worm so I just repeat "Get out!" and he slinks out like a rat, saying that in Germany nobody is "going to defend me" or say something, and everyone stands around quiet and not one voice is raised as he leaves. Not one voice has the desire or the guts to speak out for him since they know in their hearts that he was truly a rotten influence.

Of course, Rufus, not wishing to feel that he could not in some way support his colleague, says he was not alone in his problem. Naturally people can't breathe here without 'problems' but 'problems', I say to Rufus, are natural, we all have them and we will deal with them but not make problems the reason for enmity, hatred or obstruction. I then address the company standing around — their actual scenes really work and you could see theirs was one of the sections of the play that really moved forward. I have a theory that the actor playing the Tribune was even unconsciously showing fear of his partner's greater energy and attack in the part. He was clearly overshadowed by the East German. He often made references that his 'partner' did not understand, since his English was so poor, when it was clear to me that not only did his other half understand, but understood too well and was creating an interesting 'clownish villain' while he continued to look dull and grey and it occurs to me that perhaps he was angling to be sacked. I, curiously not unlike Coriolanus, blew my stack at the Tribune. He finally leaves and I immediately replace him with one of the citizens who appears pleased but acts a tad put-upon so as not to make one man's misfortunes his opportunity. He works the scene and is equally effective.

We start again with the explosion of the citizens and it is exciting to watch. The day works well now that the source of the trouble has been removed and it feels like a defective cylinder in a car has been replaced.

Volumnia, the warm-hearted Lola, can hardly remember anything and consequently we spend an inordinate amount of time repeating the lines over and over again, not to rehearse but to recall. The girl doing Valeria is at the moment hopeless and moves a bit like plasticine and the scene of the butterfly is leaden and clumsy. These are the real actresses schooled in the real theatre where directors sit and make wind with their mouths each day while the actors listen and smoke with boredom but feel that this is real because it's being discussed. It's being given weight and importance and that's why the creepo had to leave because I didn't sit for hours and talk about him and the character, and when I see this girl I see the result of that kind of verbal constipation theatre. Instead of doing an exercise to liberate and articulate she will have to listen to a three-hour lecture. I'd rather the director just said OK, let's move it, let's find out on the way. Don't describe the journey before I get there but point it out as we pass it. These actors, who can discuss the character endlessly but can't move one foot in front of the other. The poor girl tries but lacks co-ordination and her body moves in two separate sections and the voice is unconfident and quiet. Sometimes I wonder what I am doing here. She is apparently a good actress. I suppose they mean she can writhe and scream and take her clothes off. We thankfully get through the Volumnia/Virgilia sewing scene, which I think I have staged beautifully, before it's ruined by Valeria and her wooden butterfly, but I think she will improve. Sona Mac-Donald plays Virgilia with such delicate grace that I make a mental note to try to enlarge her contribution to the play.

It's evening as I write in a Japanese restaurant I have discovered called Mifune, no doubt after the great Japanese actor of the same name. I always loved this actor's earthy, powerful and comic performances in the early films of Kurosawa and not the later junk like *Ran*, praised by the critics because it reminded them of *King Lear*, while they ignored or dismissed his exquisite works like *The Hidden Fortress* as light-hearted froth when it is a masterpiece of the first order.

In the restaurant a couple sit with a child between them and both of them smoke simultaneously thus burying the child in smoke. The child already looks pale and weak. The Germans seem to give way easily to their needs. The need to smoke, complain, question — all needs they feel are their due. In New York there was an actor playing Menenius who also had a predilection to whine and a black actor playing one of the Tribunes suddenly shouted at him: "Cut out the bullshit, man" — aimed quickly like a blow. Even I was taken aback. The black actor had till now seemed quiet, smart, cool and very efficient in taking direction and making a really fascinating character, but black New Yorkers can't stand these whimpering white trash indulging in their anal masturbatory habits and it so happened he was right. Dead right. After about four weeks of playing the slob, Menenius gave in his notice because he was offered another job and thus we had to re-rehearse the whole cast to fit another Menenius in although at the time we were doing eight shows per week. Joe Papp begged him to reconsider since *Coriolanus* was a big hit and the most successful Shakespeare of the marathon, but the slob could not refuse another offer and off he went and was, of course, bad in it anyway. I wouldn't have minded that black actor out here. In New York the cast was a mix of blacks, hispanics and whites with a few Jews but here they are all Germans, although Rufus is supposed to have some Jewish blood. He certainly is an inventive actor with heaps of raw energy.

The woman on my right has ordered several strips of oily, gravied steak and gets stuck in.

The one with the real talent in the group here is, of course, the musician, Martin, who never has a problem and intuits the way into everything and hardly a word is exchanged between us. He is inspired, loves his work and is creative the way Larry Spivak in New York was, who also had no problems working with me. So people who are talented and trusting and have a way of working spontaneously have no problems . . . so what is it about the German character that seeks problems?

Again the two monsters light up their fags and the father, as he talks to the mother, blows his smoke directly in the little girl's direction and the little girl this time waves her hand to waft it away. I suppose she takes the offensive smell for granted like something about being a grown-up, as I did the rows I heard when I was a small human — trapped between two monsters.

Wednesday 26th June

Pale blue sky. Feeling terribly and achingly in love yet with a caveat attached that it's a bad match but in some ways feels the best match.

Yesterday we didn't even reach to where we had left off last Wednesday but what we are going to do is complete it. Today we must push on and try to do something with the voters' scene. Try the voters harder! Then the Tribunes with citizens and on to Act Two or the second half. Lola (Volumnia) is sadly a tad too old for this style of work and so we must try to make it easier for her since her voice is wonderful and has great power and conviction.

Today I drink too much coffee and when I get up to say something I have to remind myself that the work comes first. I have to blow away all other thoughts I have to be only, in, on, over and around the play. I mustn't let other disturbing images invade my life when I am here for these five hours and as I rise to make a statement or to show a move I have to consciously make an effort to blow my life away and live only for this. Blow away your love life, your desire or ambitions, shall I do this or that, shall I buy the studio next door, shall I divorce, remarry, fall in love? I live only for *Coriolanus* and so all my energy goes there if I am going to redirect this play and make it work again and improve and change it for Germany. In New York we sped ahead while here we seem to hold back. Not one day passes when an actor isn't sick or has to go for a performance somewhere else, which is understandable and at least reveals a healthy theatrical climate. Menenius has a performance in Dresden but I am happy with this man who sits quietly and patiently, never complains and gives an excellent performance. He waits like a Buddha, which is not to say that he is compliant and obedient for its own sake . . . he rests, watches and contributes while the other spoiled bastards from the West always need something more.

Günther continues to tell me they have 'problems' and now in my mind it's become a joke and it's not so much me any more but the text and the text doesn't match up with what I think Shakespeare says. Of course, there are some minor differences but not so enormous that they can't be solved without these huge 'problems' in the weeny voice. Before it was because I didn't sit down and explain the whole rehearsal process, which I do by showing them as we go, or, I didn't explain Roman politics versus Greek or Elizabethan, and now it's the text and soon it will be the rehearsal room, the planets, and so it goes on.

I'm in my hotel room, writing on the balcony and looking over to the woman feeding the pigeons, and I wonder about their lives. The waitress brings my breakfast like a wife . . . She saw that I didn't eat the egg yesterday so today she left it out and brought instead a huge red tomato and some tinned pineapple which she saw me eat once in the breakfast room. Is this love? It is a form of flirtation when you deliberately fix a man's tray with the things he likes. It's 26th June and we open on 13th July. Two and a half weeks to go and I could finish this easily but for the actors continually going off. I am, I must admit, in a state of continuous tension, although in some ways I enjoy Munich and wish to keep up my German lessons and so shall ask Birgitta, the costume lady, for one tonight.

Kvetch is now cast and it looks like Anita Dobson will be available after all to play the female lead. Sara Kestelman would have been superb, I know, but it was offered to Anita first and I think I shall have to go back to her even if she let it go once. I feel it is Anita's role and she will shine. I think, as she does, that Sara is the more intellectual while she is more the gutsy working class which we need. (Wicked that sometimes the things we want most in the world we are scared to have.)

We have a good day and complete more than the first half. Of course, much of it is rough but much of it is very good too. We re-do the 'voices' and try two or three at a time as it is written and it does, I confess, work better than the crowd image. Then we re-do the new Sicinius scenes with the replaced actor when he berates the citizens for giving their voice so easily and they again do the series of false exits and eventually explode out like a difficult defecation, with the aid of the Tribunes as laxatives.

We again stage the street 'fight' with Coriolanus and the Tribunes, the explosive verbal battle when he is held back like a tiger (or a rottweiler might be more appropriate). As they never seem to remember where they moved before in this complex staging we have to move it a piece at a time and achieve a strong sense of attack, withdraw, sulk, smoulder, attack and so, by a series of clashes and reactions, we stage one of those street brawls which doesn't actually get physical, not until the very end, and so by its restraint it is exciting. By what may happen, and never quite does, one fears the worst, which doesn't materialise, until the balloon goes up at the end and the help is called.

Rufus looks young and lively with his light brunette hair streaked with blond and tied into a cockscomb standing on end like it's perpetually in a state of alarm. He grows daily into the role and I watch him with interest and just sometimes with a streak of envy, when I wish I was doing it. The chorus, but for one lively middle-aged man, are young and quite fit and physical and look a lot healthier than their British counterparts. The middle-aged man has a strong piercing voice, a projection of experience and range, and leads the chorus in their doubts as the citizens who always question. One of the lads comes in and changes into his rehearsal sweat-pants and his young legs look strong. Young people don't realise how young they are. I am made aware of my age lately by all this youth around me and when I see their young hard bodies and young hairy chests I begin to think about it. I think about it now though I didn't give a damn before. I like being a middle-aged fart who looks and acts younger. I am proud of each year my being has been allowed on this earth and I should have no cause for regret, shame or comparison since I have been lucky, but when I look upon a young female face I am apt to grow a mite wistful — but that's bad values, that's cursing those great years when you threw your body round the planet like a yo-yo. So I look at the bodies of these young males and think I still have to compete with them and should not, and in fact they are not so much fitter, I say to prop up my ego, than I. I was doubting myself for the wrong reasons and perhaps because I am creeping into the lofty fifties I am finding the whole female race tantalising. It is all mental, even though each lady cycling fiercely along the Munich bike paths fills me with insufferable gloom. Their strong young thighs slashing up and down like pistons. By the end of the day I have recovered from that bout of nostalgic reverie.

We repeat the scene where the citizens come on like birds flying in to feed on corn. Coriolanus seizes one of the Tribunes, who then calls for help and, of course, this is the very provocation the Tribunes want to prove to the people his arrogance and unfittedness to rule. I enjoy the sweep and flow of the scene and how it visually and textually fits and discharges into the air a real sense of the danger to come. We move through the scene and come to the challenge, thrown by a back-to-the-wall Coriolanus to the assembled mob and again we perform our movie fight. It's not only great fun but in the swing and receive of the punch one gets rid of a lot of aggression and Rufus throws himself into it with the usual abandon. He is worrying less and enjoying it more and again the day passes smoothly without that thorn in our collective foot who was probably languishing and as it so happens making mischief like the born cur he is by going to the press.

I only have two small altercations with the cast today, one of them being the need to keep asking them to talk less since the stage manager has to ask about half a dozen times for 'start' positions. I say it wastes too much time and is not professional. The second time, when a 'complainer' goes on about the text once again and I request him to certainly air his view, but don't use it as an opportunity to 'whine'. Problems, I say, can be dealt with but not with those negative, whingey tones. Since he is a good actor and usually a 'friendly' one he takes it well and even agrees with my observation. The cast have a good giggle and like the word 'whine', which they were not familiar with and keep repeating it to him during the day and one cannot help but feel the difference in atmosphere. Everybody is relaxed and starts to push the play forward.

We reach the scene of banishment, which we stage like a trial scene with the chorus of citizens lined up on chairs like a fresco of leering accusers, whispering before Coriolanus enters and suddenly becoming silent as he walks in with Menenius, who somehow acts as his lawyer. We have just completed the scene with Mum at home when she implores him to be careful and to resist letting himself be provoked by the mob whom one should ignore. It is one of the most powerful scenes in all Shakespeare's works, a scene of utter persuasion on behalf of the mother who wishes her son to rule and imparts such wisdom, logic and sense. The mother is there and Menenius and Cominius. We cut it down to a two-hander and it was never so powerful as when we strip away those carbuncles on the side, who hang around to utter truisms. We give the lines all to Mother.

Coriolanus starts with a great rodomontade of a speech that can set the hairs on your neck bristling if you have the right actor. Rufus attacks it gamely. It is as if we catch them midway through the scene. It's worth looking at.

Let them pull all about mine ears; present me
Death on the wheel, or at wild horses' heels;
Or pile ten hills on the Tarpeian rock,
That the precipitation might down stretch
Below the beam of sight; yet will I still
Be thus to them.

This verbal chest-thump is a challenging display that Shakespeare's characters seem to like giving themselves in times of crisis and tends to display Bill's love of rhetoric and mountain-piling, and recalls Hamlet at the grave of Ophelia, talking about ". . . let them throw millions of acres on us, till our ground, singeing his pate against the burning zone, make Ossa like a wart!" It's as if he wants the character to be revealed as some kind of superman in stress, a two-fisted attack on the injustice of the world and gives the audience a chance to see the actor strut his stuff. I would have liked to see Olivier handle it and sparking sparks and he, as I was lucky to see in his *Othello*, was the one actor who could give his all and release his power or his thespian flower in such heady imagery — "like to the Propontis and the Hellespont".

When an actor has the knock-out punch these verbal arias are exciting and he will wait for this moment to soar. I can't recall many other actors in Shakespeare able to do it. I do remember Christopher Plummer doing it in a *Hamlet* which I had the good fortune to be in and to watch over twenty-five years ago. It's an art largely lost and these scenes are usually scaled down to human size and just spoken quietly as if these are subjective thoughts, since the actor has neither the equipment nor the imagination to do them. Witness Branagh's naturalistic scaling down of

Henry V compared to Olivier's soaring flights which excite listeners forty years later and is some of the greatest verse speaking of all time.

Rufus of course wishes to *cut it!* Perhaps the translation is at fault again, it usually is, but his reason is that he declares it to be *without thought!* — like it's a piece of declamatory rant and has nothing to do with the driving argument of the play. He wishes to drive the play on with the force of Coriolanus' arguments against the Tribunes and the forces against him and he feels that this speech is like a coyote howling against the wind, but of course that has magic too. But I understand too well this young German's resistance, since he hates that old-fashioned love of romantic rhetoric, flamboyant vocal actors going through the ecstasy of self-expression and bathing in their own sensual gratification. Yet Shakespeare, as we have said, liked to step off the relentless treadmill of plot and let the audience into an orgasmic howl of the character. Of course, in *Tosca*, the heroine sings one of the most moving arias in the operatic canon when faced with the iniquitous trade-off of being 'had' by the vile chief of police or having her man; she simply sings "I live for my art" and reveals the core of her being in that very moving and stirring song. So Shakespeare wished to compare the pain and torture at being trampled by wild horses' hooves as being infinitely preferable to giving in to the demands of the grovelling mob. In the end it is embarrassment that Rufus feels and the awkwardness of the modern man who flees from naked emotionalism, and while they can fight, scream and strip they find it difficult to be naked from *within*.

Our dramaturg, Günther, has given me a programme of Brecht's *Coriolan,* which I had incidentally seen at the Old Vic decades ago with the remarkable Eckhard Schall and remember his performance — titanic, rock-hard and furious. In the programme I note that there are seventy actors in the Berliner Ensemble, one for each role, while in our production we have a tight eighteen. Quite sufficient since with doubling each actor can expand his craft and range, has more to do and is, of course, more work-fulfilled. So huge is the Berliner Ensemble's cast that most of them must be backstage in the canteen getting sloshed while waiting endless hours to go on for the battle scenes. The actors will be less skilled and stagnate and be frustrated. Yet the productions were models of clarity and power and so I surmise that they must have been choreographed well to get the most out of the scenes and the players. As I remember, crowds swirled and cloaks swirled and the effect was very Roman, reminiscent of the great statues carved out of stone where the rolling layers of cloak were as much part of the personalities as the faces. In those heady days the National at the Vic would import the great companies and the theatre was more than cultural massage for tourists. It was serious, exciting business.

Looking at the Berliner programme and at the photos within I was pleased to know what they were doing in each scene. Brecht, of course, altered the play to ensure that the citizens were the oppressed workers and the heroes of the piece and Coriolanus the villain and in some way this gives it the right historic perspective. Why should the citizens who have been kept hungry wish to fight for the Roman elite just to get a bit of corn? Coriolanus spouts to the Tribunes: "they would not thread the gates", a nice metaphor for the tired, undernourished citizens who decided at some moment to spare their bodies from being cannon fodder once again.

Anyway, after all this, Rufus reluctantly tries it out. I have staged it in an odd way. Since the stage is supposed to be black and white squares I put each actor in his own square as if trapped in his own thoughts and neither giving way: like four chess pieces. Each square is lit. The effect is of a zoo or pet shop with each animal in its own cage and yet adjacent and visible to each other. Menenius is brought on early and he paces as in an empty room. Then Cominius comes on and he occupies his square. It looks effective and gives the feeling of cells. Coriolanus is in another square and Volumnia in the last one. They conduct the scene with all its arguments in isolation until Coriolanus gives in to reason with the Tribunes and accepts the directions from Mum to be 'mild' and they finally break down the barriers and converge in one square. It feels and looks good. We reach the more-than-halfway stage when the interval will come and there is a marked relief from everyone. Even I feel good. Nearly three weeks to go. The sun warms me as I leave the rehearsal room and I take a cab to the food market, which is one of my favourite haunts, and eat a chicken noodle soup.

Thursday 27th June

We get on the stage today for the first time. The stage area down to the rake has been constructed for us to rehearse on and we throw what we have created in the hothouse of the rehearsal room on to the vast open auditorium. Suddenly everyone starts overacting as if to compensate for the back wall being 100 feet away instead of just in front of their noses. The play seems full of choral effects, shouts, declamations. The noise is deafening, from the floorboards echoing the footsteps to everyone talking at once whenever we stop even for a few seconds.

As Lola comes in the actors feel they have to hug everyone and gossip about what has happened since they saw each other the night before. I like the way an oriental actor enters the stage or a gym. He bows to the space and begins, whereas here the stage is just an extension of their social life. It's a pity they can't do it in the canteen.

In the stalls the stage managers are talking and now tell me Menenius won't be here today, in fact not till Monday, and today is Thursday. They swear they told me about this time off weeks ago. How on earth am I supposed to carry all this in my head without an efficient organisation to remind me days earlier or even the previous day, so one can reorganise rehearsals or keep a rehearsal calendar that can be modified when necessary? Not to be reminded the day before but to expect the director to create and remember and keep notes of every piece of shit they tell me. Well, this is the famous German efficiency and I'm beginning to see through it. It is less efficiently run than the sloppy, under-subsidised Public Theater in New York. Less efficient than a lunch time at the King's Head. In New York they were so on the ball and didn't miss a trick. Here the girls are bright and alert but seem to be 'learning' or 'students'. They have largely come from university and therefore are hopeless about the rude practicalities of running a prompt corner or stage-managing, although they did make a comment that surprised me. It is my habit to ask the nearest eyes next to me how it looks, or if this or that works, and hope for a good response for or against, a kind of instantaneous feedback. Well, one of them confessed that never in the two or more years she had worked there had any director so much as spoken to them, let alone asked their opinions! Well, more fool them, since the people next to you are eyes, ears and noses and their gut response can be very accurate when you might, as a director, go a bit askew or travel up your own arse. Anyway, they blithely reiterate that they told me, expecting me to retain all information and take responsibility on the scheduling which should be theirs. So we stupidly have to start the scene again with the Tribunes and the vital part missing. Eventually we cancel it and instead return to some of our battle sequences and by repetition they now seem to overwhelm the play, but in fact they don't.

Next we rehearse the rabble racing on complaining and then defending their Tribunes. Then we do the chess piece scene in the squares, which works very well and has an eerie feel to it: in the end we will cut Menenius from it since his continual absences give me the idea of turning it into a two-hander and so from tribulation come bonuses. In fact, I have a theory that strife and tribulation actually are the other side of the coin of success, illumination and achievement. Each little mess I have got myself into produced its after-effect, which was some revelation of the pain. The last scene, when Coriolanus is exiled, now has the chorus as a shouting fresco of faces silently mouthing their contempt as they shove their little grimy fists in the air. It's as if we view them with the sound turned off while Coriolanus makes his speech of contempt ending in "I banish you!" Suddenly the rehearsal must come to an end as we are allowed the stage for three hours only and must return to the hot, and now unpleasant by contrast, rehearsal room. Again the stage manager limply walks around reading in Menenius and, of course, can't help it for a minute that she not only doesn't sound like our East German actor but acts like a wet lettuce from university who has had a privileged existence all her life and wears smart clothes to rehearsal. No wonder the theatre absolutely needs eight and more weeks to rehearse a play, which isn't so long except that I have done it before, and much of the investigation of a production is how it's staged.

The action on the stage feels OK and the exits and entrances work well. Another actor has replaced Karlheinz (Titus Lartius), whoever he is, since Karlheinz had trouble with his leg and the new Titus walks through his part like the living dead. After he left I wickedly allowed myself a stab of impersonation and the cast admit that he could "scare them to death" if he couldn't awe them with his power. In other words, I imagine they mean his 'ghostly' presence. Cominius is beginning to grow on me and has a good, stately Roman presence with his chiselled German officer look and steely grey hair. Rufus has now established a Freudian interpretation and wails a mite too often, especially during his scene with Mum, and he hits the notes with a sledgehammer where it indicates another fixation. It should be more on the line of Jimmy Cagney in *White Heat*, although the sobbing, floor-clinging seems to suit him. Lola is now very good in the scene but a little tired. Menenius, when he is here, is a first-class speaker, but none of them seem to remember a move and on each line they keep looking to the stage manager to tell them where they move as if we hadn't repeated the scene at least twelve times. Your moves dictate who you are and what your impulses are and so to forget means you are not interested in the structure but only in the character and the 'lines'. When I was acting for others in rep the moves were crucial to my releasing of the role. Rufus improvises moves well and is very graceful and forceful but most of them seem unable to absorb moves into their bodies unless the scene is 'deliberately choreographed' but the chorus is very good and the ensemble work is tightening and the team are getting a 'team' spirit and growing day by day.

Hans, one of the 'pretty' actors who wears a cute earring each day, tells me that he thinks we are shouting too much — that's because the group scenes are the only ones we do when the actors are away so much — but there is a repetition on words that we should watch out for, but they are usually when the citizens are roused and join in a chant to banish him or the greetings when Coriolanus returns from Rome and we repeat his name as a kind of ritual celebration. Hans never says anything that is not a criticism or concern and his concerns are genuine, but there is never anything positive that he comes out with. It's again a kind of whiny dirge. Perhaps he has been spoiled by his women and is used to receiving. Terrible to be handsome and spoiled since you never really develop the muscles that are used for giving, they are too weak. He was absent one day, ill, he says, and couldn't even bring himself to apologise to me for his absence. Like it didn't matter that we had to work round him. However, the actors are giving a lot more, particularly Tom, the older man, who never for a second stints in his contribution and seems to genuinely like what he is doing. In an ensemble, each link is vital to the whole, unlike your average Shakespeare where it doesn't matter a fart whether you're alive or dead as long as the principals are there. For British groups the idea of ensemble and collecting the energy of the mass is as foreign as the Aztec language. Ensemble is also brotherhood and unity. It carries the power of the play and invigorates the audience.

So far the play works but at night loneliness eats into the soul and starts to chew away at the edges.

Friday 28th June

Work knocks the shit out of you and tonight we work but there is not much time left. A whole week to do the second, shorter half and we could do it easily if the actors didn't keep fiddling with the text to make it suit their modern tastes. My maudlin mood is broken by getting right up to the Aufidius scene when he greets Coriolanus in exile. It works well. So we're eating into it and by next Wednesday we should have completed the plotting. Must keep temper. Lose it tonight with my lady assistant. I am again told of a missing actor. Just cool it.

The scene when Coriolanus greets Aufidius is full of mine-fields for Rufus. He feels awkward in these shows of 'affection' and I remember Chris Walken in New York felt something similar. Men seem to be so embarrassed by expressing emotion and I have never seen it quite so much as in recent years. It should be a love tryst. A pact. A scene of passion when each man sees the mirror of himself. Narcissus. Each strong, rebellious, brave. Macho and admiring the courage of each other. It may be difficult for Rufus since Aufidius is hardly wolf-like but is rather a pleasant German who resembles a blacksmith in a country village and is apt to make a flinging arm gesture as if he might break into 'Maid of the Mountains'. My old ally, German actor Wolf Kahler, would have been a good Aufidius. The black actor, Keith David, in New York was a perfect Aufidius. Strong, funny, big-hearted, rebellious and sinister by turns. He gave Walken a run for his money and rather stole the thunder. When he held Chris Walken he engulfed his whole body with his huge arms and Chris allowed himself to be passively held and couldn't respond. I saw the scene in my mind as a kind of dance of joy, a series of rondos, holding, gripping, squeezing, playing but now we make it quiet and serious to accommodate the emotions of the German actors, a rather mock intensity, and it also works well. The other way, Rufus feels, is a bit of a cliché.

We do the scene so often that I resolve that this is the last time. We'll work more at night since it's like a kind of bonus time and you achieve a lot because the pressure of achievement necessary during the day is lifted. As long as we have a clear week of runs we are OK, in good shape. Aufidius is a good man with a good heart but he can't seem to put it into his work, whereas Rufus has style but not so much heart at the moment and so the scene doesn't yet have the warmth or the ambiguity that it needs. (Don't waste your Friday night with the fantasy of returning to the UK, but work.)

I leave and it is getting dark and I decide to look into a Weinstube. The candles are lit, the tables warm-hearted and cosy, the food ready for you — so different from the squalor of England and its wine bars and pubs. The counter is wooden and clean and has no stink of beer or urine. A coffee machine sits in the corner gleaming and ready to give you a delicious espresso. The atmosphere is so warm, clean and ordered it looks almost Zen-like.

I order a Beaujolais and it comes in a large wine glass and sinks into me in all the right places. I feel ecstatic. I reflect: the first act is going to be OK apart from some dead wood in some minor parts but it flows. The second can't seem to get locomotion but we have ploughed through the first three scenes. Saturday? Rehearse. Why should I kill myself for them? But I feel it will make life easier at the end. These weekend breaks to London have been my godsend. But not always. Aufidius bothers me since he is so miscast, but he will improve and has great willing. They have no understudies here as they do at the National, can you believe it! And so if a principal is sick they just cancel the show! So much for the myth of the great German theatre. I suggest understudy rehearsal as we have in the UK since it gives the producer a chance to test actors out and the actors, of course, a chance to play lead parts and I want to see Wolfgang Bauer try Aufidius and then he gets a chance to put the virus of the role into his bloodstream. Then on the days off they can rehearse. In New York when Aufidius was off, Roger Smith came in and revealed himself as the actor I had never ever suspected. It's vital, necessary and is the best use of the manpower you are paying. Train them, for God's sake, and they would not whine and complain so much like a lot of under-used old ladies. No disrespect to old ladies! Unbelievably, Günther, the Intendant, says they *never* considered such a thing! Never considered the obvious method that would prevent cancellations, money being wasted and give nourishment to the actors. Nothing! I could have said we must all sit naked in the middle of the city. Which is, ironically, what the natives do here on the weekend in their parks.

The sky tonight is a deep, clear, icy blue and I walk down the road and fall into my next comfort station, the Chinese restaurant, which is strangely attached to the Stück museum and I can't imagine a more perfect atmosphere to sit and write, and the food is wonderful. As I eat my chicken noodles and bean sprouts I let my mind wander round the globe. We all have our globes and make visits here and there. Dip into the various islands of our past. It is a tranquil time away from the world's cares. My spirit likes to take off — commonly called daydreaming like a wistful drifting — but I think of it as creative pioneering. It is the one area where we are free to transport ourselves into the loveliest places on earth and I know where I head for. It is to be with someone you care about, to love those mood-caressing moments that bring you closer to the inner part of yourself which may be called your soul . . . soul food . . . after two sakis and my lovely noodles I am ready to crash.

Saturday 29th June

Disturbed night. Bad dreams. Woke as if I was feeling by telepathy some disquiet miles away. Can't discuss it.

The play seems to creak on, with absentees making it longer, and the dreary stage management crew. But we do some good work and fill in the end. We do the death scene and block the scene when Volumnia comes to beg Coriolanus to stop the invasion of Rome. Rufus again seems reluctant to take the emotion out of his heart and put it on the stage: "O, mother, mother, what have you done?" In one of the few directions we attribute to Shakespeare it states: "He takes her hand", her small, withered old hand is taken by her warrior son — the actor should cry, he must. He hears her begging, pleading in a prostrate position on the floor, but more than this he sees his old, stately mother on her knees. Rufus walks over to her like it was a stage direction. Unmoved, not a sign of yielding to the creature that has moulded him. Even the text says: ". . . it is no little thing to make mine eyes sweat with compassion." It's a release, a breaking down of the fortress, of opening the door. He sees his mother begging for life, freedom from war, and he must feel like a bad boy who has broken something precious and now must come to Ma for forgiveness. The child must break through all the encrustations of manhood, through all the layers of muscle and be the boy again. Cry. (I cry so easily these days.) I suggest to Rufus that he should cover his face and weep — "O, mother. . .", he says — go over to her, I think, and amaze yourself by the sudden eruption of your own passions . . . feel foolishly but deliriously liberated. Show you have been touched. Feel! We've had enough of all the bullshit macho posing, now let's see some real emotion and a real man crying. A dead man can't cry.

Aufidius makes the point that their battles are like a love tryst. Witness the weakness of Coriolanus' wife when she fears the wounds that may afflict her husband. She can only feebly lament: "O Jupiter! no blood." Contrast Aufidius' great outpourings: "Let me twine mine arms about that body. . ." etc., etc. And again to Coriolanus he raves: "But that I see thee here, thou noble thing! more dances my rapt heart than when I first my wedded mistress saw. . ." And then further: "I have nightly since dreamt of encounters 'twixt thyself and me: we have been down together in my sleep, unbuckling helms, fisting each other's throat, and wak'd half dead with nothing." Bold words in an anti-homo age. A little disguise goes a long way. So here Shakespeare paints a picture of two men at war with each other, killing each other's citizens and yet after each blood-letting jolly good pals once again, while the dead push up the daisies. It's a bit Boy's Own and smacks of much macho exclusivity and the theme of the great punch-ups is over-stressed with poetic imagery and phoney hero-ism. Mentioned just once too often. So here we have the hard boy homosexual closeted mother-fucker, in a word. But we won't in the mother's scene achieve this breakdown nor any real emotion in the scene with Aufidius.

I detect an embarrassment among the Germans to show emotion, as I have said, and Rufus makes jokes about it before doing the lines as if he found it all a bit over the top or soppy. Chris Walken, coincidentally, found it equally awkward to be one moment macho and the next vulnerable, open, sensitive or emotional. But shout he could. Curiously, Walken is of German descent. The modern man has become cool. Remote. An iceberg. It seems like it's the older ones that can let it all hang out. I remember saying to Barry Philips, who was playing Laertes in my production of *Hamlet*: "Get down on the floor and weep your heart out", and he did that very thing without so much as questioning it. I suppose he trusted me. I shall never forget him doing that. He fell to his knees over Ophelia's body and heaved, cried. We all tried crying after him so that he should not feel alone and then when Terry McGinity took over the role he followed Barry and wept his heart out. I have never seen actors do this before or since. Usually it's a quick brush of the wrist over imaginary tears.

Monday 1st July

Today I return from London, where I went for the weekend to rehearse *The Tell-tale Heart*, which I am recording a week after *Coriolanus* finishes. We used as a location an old synagogue in Brick Lane, which is now a kind of museum — one of those synagogues which sprang up in the early nineteenth century in a house when there were not enough actual buildings of worship. The house had been gutted and became this beautiful old temple. I try recalling the congregation praying here a hundred years ago. It's old and dusty and reeks of atmosphere and reminds me of the old Half Moon Theatre, which was also a synagogue, where my play *Greek* first appeared in London in 1980 after its small work-out in Croydon's tiny Warehouse Theatre. At the old Half Moon I sat and watched *Greek* unfold from the balcony which used to separate the sexes during prayer. Quite rightly too. How could a man concentrate with the perfumed flesh of his wife or beloved near him? How could he devote himself to the word while hearing the breath of his lady or her swishing petticoats? He would be torn between the world of the spirit and the earth, both holy, both vital, but one cannot serve two gods simultaneously and so, wisely, the women were placed upstairs so that they might watch and hover over the men like angels. So, in that hot empty dusty synagogue I unfurled my testament of murder. Poe's *The Tell-tale Heart* . . . We staged it for TV as if it were in a kind of court, in front of an examining magistrate. I was exhausted and fled home and crashed out after an Indian meal with C at the Mala in St Katharine Docks.

Get up at 6am and tear down to Heathrow, which is chock-a-block. It gets worse and worse but soon I am on my cool

silver capsule, staring somewhat lamely at the BA magazine, with its anodyne coverage of the world and an article
about Mexico dying in a cloud of poisonous smog, growing
worse daily, and the millions who live in filthy tin shacks
made out of empty gasoline canisters. I sit in club class,
and beneath me the world looks calm as the sun breaks
through; a river snakes through the land and a forest looks
dark and green and the sky a washed blue. All is at peace
in Germany devoid of too much Catholic bullying. The
plane lands with a gentle squish and a taxi waits at the
airport. We glide along the sun-filled Munich streets so
bitterly contrasted with the grey wash we have left behind
in England. My hotel, all cosily Bavarian, greets me, clean,
calm and collected.

I walk swiftly to the theatre to find that the stage management hasn't called the actors for the beginning of the
second half because Virgilia (small part) isn't there! Virgilia has about two lines in the scene and not so much
'business' and so in the end they cancel a vital scene
which needs to be plotted. These people are impossible
and any relationship to stage management in England and
this lot is purely coincidental. I don't even think they
regard themselves as stage management but elevate themselves as 'assistants' to the director. Some assistants! I feel
like going for a walk but in the end we do other scenes and
work with Lola.

Rufus grows more and more confident but has developed a
tinge of a whine and now plays sulkily and a little hard
done by, too much the spoiled boy. His long El Greco face
wanders into rehearsals with its headband on and seldom
offers much greeting but at least he gets on with it. The
annoying thing is that as he grows confident he is always
making directorial suggestions, which I have to try to listen
to and then veto. He also sees a way of avoiding emotional
scenes by 'stylising' them. Reality, he feels, is old-fash-

ioned and while style is appropriate for the production there have to be scenes of real emotional and visceral power. There seems to be little variation in tone, even allowing for the fact that I don't understand the language — straight po-faced or rising tenor shout. However, he is growing and will no doubt add colour later. To be with these guys for five hours requires me in many ways to be a creature like the winter hedgehog that feeds upon itself. I think I have stored enough within me to be self-sufficient to a point. So when the scene works, having no feedback, I just congratulate myself!

When it works well I am aglow. When the day ends I say to the cast or stage management it was a good day, and we plotted several scenes, even with detail, and we still have ten days. Then some prissy tart says: "Ja, but what about the detail?" As if all this work, sweat, toil, choreography, invention, innovation was not enough. As if they can't squeeze one ounce of positive thought from their dried-up, tight-arsed little bodies. So like Volumnia who says, when asked to sup with Menenius: "Anger's my meat; I sup upon myself . . ."

So I find that it's working well and even improving on the well-received New York production and the team are growing daily in spirit and becoming a worthy ensemble. My shaven-headed Wolfgang senses my reliance on his unique physical presence and gives his all to each of his parts. In fact he would have made a splendid Aufidius if not a future Coriolanus.

So, after the absence of Tom the elder citizen with an eye injury, we get to the end, including the *coup de grâce*, which is the attaché case. This particular biz happened in New York when Coriolanus comes to make his peace with Aufidius. I have Cominius open a small black attaché case and deliver the familiar manilla envelope containing peace proposals. Aufidius takes the envelope with the tip of his fingers as if it were something disgusting and tosses it away contemptuously. Coriolanus is murdered and his body removed. Cominius is left on stage and picks up the envelope and places it back in the case and while kneeling on one knee slams the case shut to the accompaniment of a drum beat which Martin smashes down. The lights go out. Peace is extinguished forever. It's such a moving and dramatic ending since it emphasises not Coriolanus' death and his body being carried out in the best heroic tradition but with the ending of peace and the slamming shut of a small simple case. The hope of mankind is shut up in the darkness of the case.

We are now nearly finished and have to light the thing as the next ordeal. The theatre closes for two days to allow time for set, lights and technical. Not too much time with the crew, as I will find out.

Ten days before opening. I'm happy. I am always happy at the end of a day's work. I feel uplifted and my personal difficulties shrivel momentarily.

After work I follow my familiar route. Now I have a kind of tea break at 5.30 in the Kafer deli. This is an ornate mini-Harrods with the best of everything on several floors and a small café-restaurant where you can order anything of the endless variety of things you see in the grocery store. Passing the greengrocery section, I decide on arugula salad with Parmesan cheese and tomatoes. It arrives without much delay with a selection of the most incredible Italian leaves and thinly shaved slices of Parmesan and tiny delicious tomatoes adorning the plate, like it was studded in ceramics. Then I call home and feel desperately alienated. It is hot and I lie on the bed once more and think about the world. What is there for me in the world out there?

Tuesday 2nd July

It's hot . . . run round the park, sweat and send my daily fax. So glad to have my typewriter. Sweated in the night and dreamed of a lunatic forcing a glass down a girl's throat and somehow I could not make him let go. What does this mean? Must analyse it.

I walk to work and run the second half. It flows easily and some looks very good. Menenius yet again has had to go to do a show in Dresden and Tom is still away with his bad eye. Sona is in Paris doing her show at the Odéon and so each scene has a problem with an absentee, bar one with Aufidius. At least we can now run through it and we are ahead of the game by ten days. Bravo.

I have changed the scene with Volumnia's plea to Coriolanus not to invade Rome, which is another of those famous set pieces. Originally I plotted it with the mother trailing Coriolanus and when she got close to his stiff, recalcitrant figure, he'd move away so, both physically and emotionally, he wished there to be no contact. I wanted her walk to be slow, arduous, a bit like Mother Courage. She has travelled many miles to make her plea and is worn out. She approaches him and sadistically he turns away and the process must begin again. When she breaks through his defences he is distraught, abject and in grief breaks down and weeps (though Rufus merely wipes his dry eyes). Now I feel that Coriolanus should stand rock still and move not an inch while Mother haunts his ear and his wife Virgilia, played by the clever Sona, haunts and crawls round his body almost like a snake. He is like a statue but gradually turns into a human being and then he cries, but not yet of course, and not here. It is a new way and works wondrously. Sona very slowly weaves her way down his cold, hard form, melting it a bit as she grows lissom, a kind of fire over a statue of ice. She kneels at his feet and places her cheek on his shoe. She humbles herself slowly, inevitably insinuating herself around him like a perfume or a drug. The mother continues to win his ear and so between them, acting on mind and body, they will surely make him crumble and it's unique and one of the best things I have done and everybody loves it. It is also very sexy. Rufus makes his last speech strong, clear and tense, like an eagle about to spring. This death is so much better than the weird one Walken opted for in the mimed execution by spears and the final *coup de grâce* by Aufidius and at last I see it work.

We finish early and satisfied. As I am working in the theatre tonight with the lights I take a soup in the canteen. I am so empty, sad and sorrowful that I lead the actor in the canteen to tell me about his private life. He is a nice chap with a pony tail. "Has he a girlfriend?" Such thoughts transfix me at the moment. He says, "No . . . not at the moment", but six months ago his girlfriend of four years broke up with him. He tells me he was demolished. So refreshing to see that a man can feel so much. I recall a girlfriend of mine leaving me after four years to run away with my Polish lodger. I too was distraught before I realised she was doing me a favour. I am happy to have found a male who so readily confesses his pain. He is a nice, carefree fellow and tells me he wanted to play Coriolanus. He is very funny and clever in what he does in the play, chiefly as leading citizen. He is agreeable and pleasant. I go back to the rehearsal room to work with Rufus and Lola. "Where are you off to now?" I ask at the end of rehearsal, hoping maybe he'd like a drink. Back to his family of two kids he said. He lives with a woman but is not married. Perhaps he found it difficult to make such a public gesture of his love when he has trouble doing it in the play.

I am 'forced' into the theatre to do lights. By 'forced' I mean it has suddenly been thrust upon me to plot them, when I hadn't even been told to work out the plot in advance with the lighting technician. We haven't finished rehearsing and suddenly I'm in the theatre with a bunch of people *who haven't even seen a run-through!* There appears to be no stage management and my assistants have no real idea of production procedure. I have simply been asked to light as the theatre is closed tonight. We continue our rehearsal on stage and so the lighting man is at least able to see that. Apparently it's rare in this theatre for lighting to be used as an integral part of the action. It's just there to view the actors and nothing more.

So, we finish Act Two amidst Rufus' constant kvetching now, about nearly every scene he is in, but I attribute this to nerves, since we're now on stage and the first night approaches. The reality of the play draws nigh. Rufus seems to be working on anger all the time and will now not be balanced unless he relieves himself with a show of tenderness. The blonde stage manager who works the corner and the lights says "*You* should play Coriolanus", and it makes me feel a hell of a lot better and I think: "Why not?"

I am told or informed by Günther that I should 'try' one or two cues for the lights. Naturally there are two actors missing and so the rest run as best they can but the stage floor impedes all their movement and catches their shoes. It's appalling. Utterly detestable. Square slabs of polystyrene that you trip over and these same squares are held together by small metal plates that keep coming loose and carpenters keep running on to rescrew the plates back. This is the great German theatre. So I let the actors come on and get used to the stage and test their voices and Günther sits behind me, squirming and repeating, "Why don't you give the lighting man some cues?" and starts behaving like some bureaucrat in the Third Reich. "Why don't you tell them when there is a scene change?" I tell him that the lighting plot and the establishing of the design has hardly begun and since we have so little time in the theatre it would be a waste of time to do it now. There are no areas lit. I need to be in the theatre for a whole day to focus. Not just a quick couple of hours in the evening. You have to try it out first with stand-ins and establish the areas. We haven't done anything of this.

Still Günther keeps shrieking behind me, thus proving he is the authoritarian I always believed him to be and not the benign nice guy he tries to convey to the actors. He is now trying to establish his authority and actually telling me off in front of the actors, which is the most thoughtless behaviour a producer could be capable of and destined to make for an explosion. At the moment I can't even be bothered to lose my rag. At least he can't have me shot. So he's telling me off, saying that we must save time, while he is wasting it and bringing the rehearsal to a standstill. He appears to have little idea of production procedure or at least has no idea of mine, which is to be very cool and get it down to the bare bones. I am not one for those hysterical all-night sessions so beloved of British directors with their revolves that don't work and endless scene changes. They don't feel as if they have worked unless it's full of torture, mishaps, costume failures. This very week in an entertaining diary piece in the *Guardian* the distinguished director Mike Bogdanov refers to the torture of the first night of *The Ginger Man* in Hamburg where he is leaving after a directorship of some years. He is up all night with the sets in chaos and everything is fraught with confusion. I could never admit to this; it would be like admitting that your army is in disarray and your troops killed, but never mind, he says, it's all in the night's work. A bottle of Scotch and all will be well. This kind of set, costume, effects-clotted method of the Brits always surprises me and how they seem to need the torture since they try to bring together elements that don't work in a couple or three days. In the end Bogdanov said of his first night that he couldn't even watch it — but hears the applause from offstage. Coward! You should be there with your troops on the first night to celebrate their victory. The fucking actors have to be there. I am always very proud to be there on the first night because I know it will go like a dream. It will be organic and simple and based on the skills of the performers and not on the temperament of a set change, pulleys, revolves or descending junk. However, we are all different, but I have heard this "I couldn't watch it" many times, both from writers and directors, but I say, stay and watch and suffer the torture you inflict on others.

Sometimes it is easier to be on the stage than to watch. The set is awful, the cyclorama hasn't improved, the stage manager keeps saying she is not a stage manager and that the method is different here in Germany than in England and the one stage manager for real is in the corner and can never see me. There seems to be nobody in charge of the book of the play except the blonde ex-dancer who cues the lights. So she is the real stage manager. The missing link. Eventually Günther storms out in a bubble of hysteria and we get on with it calmly.

Tomorrow I will have all day to deal with the lights and set without the actors so we'll move forward. They can run it by themselves in the rehearsal room and whine and complain all they like. I've frankly had enough.

After work I crawl into the little bar opposite with Dieter, Günther's assistant, and he is civilised, charming and cultivated. This is a German pub, Dieter tells me. Well, you could have fooled me. I order the most perfect pasta with salmon and two glasses of red wine. "What time do you close?" I casually enquire. "4am — but only eating until 3am!" Again I think of our lazy brewers' stinking pubs, slovenly dirty, rancid and ungovernably depressing with the gormless chewing their crisps at the bar and the contrast with this, which, as I said before, is like a Zen temple.

Wednesday 3rd July

We're back in the torture chamber of the theatre, so maybe they run pubs better than theatres. Every cue I call out has to be translated by this amateur assistant trying to describe it in her nice way, but since she is not of the theatre she knows no technical words and tries to convey them in her layman's tongue and I start to force back the contempt I feel for these privileged university tarts who love the theatre and the drama, 'darling'. I hate the endless sitting around waiting for the cue and decide to scrub the colours and stick to white light.

The only peace here is in the canteen and I indulge myself with a pair of Vienna sausages. Delicious. They taste crunchy and good. Instead of work being a pleasure, here it is next to hell. And we still have another week of it! So do it slowly. Longing for company. So the weekends have it.

A production assistant has just come in and we are working like a team at last. The young man is efficient, with a deadly earnestness about him, and seeks to prove his worthiness. He gets into the swing of things and when our swarthy lighting rigger sounds a touch obstreperous my young blond efficient assistant screams at him like the best Ersatzgruppenführer. Now I am in business and am free at last from this woman who has plagued me with her incompetence ever since I have been here — but she means well and was probably chosen as much for her excellent command of English as anything else. But she has also made my work that much harder.

Günther calls me into his office and is obviously on a hysteria binge. The adrenalin can make some people seek these outlets as if a drug. It courses through and makes you feel stronger. He seems to enjoy hearing his own voice. Remarkably in this instant I go for super-cool response and try diplomacy. I have found that the cast have behaved stupidly and sulkily but on reflection I realise that it is Günther's attitude that has unmanned them. When he made his inane comments about giving the lighting man cues when the lights weren't fixed up, this caused great consternation amongst the cast because they believed that the hotch-potch of lights that was thrown up, or rather vomited up, was what we were having and so, of course, there was panic this morning when they had to rehearse alone while I continued doing the 'real' lights with my new efficient assistant. My new assistant's outburst to the lighting man impressed me no end because it was filled with hate and we had only just begun.

Back in the office Günther talks of everything from the problems with the text, the people, to absentees, and to me having a Saturday morning off. His voice drones on and I have to have a fag — a Samson roll-up — and drink a coffee. He is talking of cancelling some of the other shows so we can open on time. Of course, it's a practice that is routine at the National Theatre to keep a theatre dark for up to five days so that you have the time for an ambitious lighting rig. Here they don't close the theatre but expect you to fill in in the afternoons and then get chucked out at 4pm so that they can put the set back.

Again I feel alien as he stirs the shit with his tongue and makes me hate the actors, unnecessarily as it happens. "They're all very unhappy", he moans. I think of the unhappy actors. I think of Lola, to whom I have given so much time and energy, walking her through her lines, demonstrating when she had problems, giving her marvellous business to do, encouraging her, praising: this old actress, who can't remember her moves, says she is unhappy. Of course, I know that Rufus is, but he always is and that's the way he winds up his energy and so he is part of the problem. In that, *they* are the problem but wish to transfer their incompetence to me. I felt the actors were beginning to enjoy and understand the style of work until Günther, probably meaning well, bungled and tainted the atmosphere. I imagine myself in club class, drinking champagne rather than suffering this torture over a production that was not only far better by miles than anything I had seen in Munich but in fact was on the way, was working well and looked very good. It was a lot of fart for nothing. Dieter, who had walked outside with me, took me by the hand and said: *"I'm* with you," and I knew him to be a good human being and I knew that all is not lost when such men are around.

How all actors club together like mutineers against the captain, but they are not really hostile except when they are inflamed by the nerves of one who infects the ready-to-be-inflamed nerves of the others. Doubt spreads like a contagion in the doubtful performer with the first night looming up, but I know that it will work and work well and that is why it angers me all the more that Günther, instead of pouring oil on troubled waters as all good producers should, pours oil on the fire.

This afternoon I go to the English Garden, which is now my regular haunt, and have a mixed salad and sit in the sun amidst hundreds of happy people. The café is a cornu-copia of everything you could want and sausages are frying and sizzling and sold by the thousand. People drink from huge steins of beer and eat brown bread, chopped carrots and cheese or even bring their own food. A Peruvian group of musicians is playing in the garden and the men are pure Indian, with beautiful broad faces and long black hair.

Ring Rufus when I get back and I am spoiling for a fight and want to know why he complains so much when I have given him so much of my time and energy and why he has to go to Günther rather than talk to me. We meet in the canteen and my sails are slackened somewhat by his con-trite attitude and his genuine worry, and so we talk about his childhood and his boarding school days where he would go to the loo to cry since you couldn't do it in front of your colleagues or show your feelings. It gives me an insight into why he always wishes to stylise feelings rather than nakedly express them and I am grateful for his shar-ing a little of his life with me.

We go into the rehearsal room and I suddenly feel guilty for writing negatively about his contribution, because nega-tive feelings have to be listened to with care and attention and not always thought of as antagonism to me. Although of course there are limits! And I am feeling guilty because, in some ways, what transpires between director and actors is a pact of confidentiality and you take advantage because you are able to write about it and then publish from your point of view. Many of Rufus' thoughts are concise and clear. I had in the New York production to pacify Chris Walken, who rushed on so he could get the 'overview' he was so keen on, and my way of working is in slow detail.

I worked fast through certain sections in the New York production so that I could get to Coriolanus' scenes. Now Rufus may have inherited some of the congealed wodge and with his sharp intelligence sees there is more in the scene than I had worked out with Walken. So in each scene he is unravelling the details and revealing to me more than I had seen before. Thus the greeting with the senators in the first scene should savour more of the ritual of power than the Boy's Own 'let's have a punch-up' we had in New York. Rufus felt that men of this authority and power would not just meet and chat but have some kind of sign, some naturalistic salute that denoted their position. So we devise something and it works and makes the scene richer. It is a small thing but it has resonance, it is one of those signs expressed in a hand-clasp, the kind of greeting our black cousins have as a clan sign and demonstration of solidarity. It makes an event of something I was willing to gloss over. I, who pride myself in having such an eye for detail, have run roughshod over some scenes, creating my own choreographic razzmatazz and not zoning in to those areas that didn't seem to need attention. My mind was probably leaping on hot coals over events in Blighty and I had holes in the work in hand. Now I shall repair them all.

We improve Coriolanus' first entrance by making it slow and threatening. We also improve the scene for Lola so that she sits down while Coriolanus dances round her. Now she has something real to get her teeth into. Mind you, in the end we go back to my squares of light but in reducing them to two the contestants battle it out and it is very powerful.

We examine the scene where Coriolanus comes in like a rag doll and finds his troops, who are exhausted from battle. Before, we had the soldiers perform the usual exclamation of eurekas on seeing their General, but now the real way is that they can barely stand up. He rallies them but they fall again with fatigue; in the end they pick themselves up when he asks for volunteers who value their country more than themselves and slowly they build themselves once more by his persuasion into a fighting group. We have now put our noses more into the potential of the scene which in New York I didn't feel I was allowed time to do — and my own nose has been thrust into my own sorry and pathetic stew. Rufus' fears were real and his examination cast a light over my own shortcomings. You cannot worship two wives. Arbeit über Alles.

Even Günther peeks in to see how the two adversaries are getting on, a bit like Mum, and I feel a little mean about what I had scrawled in anger. Günther only expresses the feelings of his company whom he seeks to protect, although I still think his interference was maladroit, but let's not dwell on it or I shall give myself more heartaches and crossings out.

Go to the Ludwigstrasse to meet Sona after her performance in the Kammerspiel Theatre and we sit and chat, drink wine and eat a pasta and I start to feel human again. The theatre is next to the café. The photos in the vestibule look exciting. In Munich it is the favoured theatre while ours is usually condemned by the critics for no better reason than the fact that they don't seem to like the Intendant, Günther Beelitz.

Sona tells me about her one-woman show in Paris and is awash with Parisian impressions. She is glowing after her show in the little studio which seats fifty people. Günther had been to see her as he frequently checks up on the shows. How unlike our British directors, who hardly ever look in after the first night.

Strange dream about women. Seemingly I had an affair with some small blonde who had red-rimmed puffy eyes . . . who was that? Not C. C is pretty and sometimes looks like a child and is funny. There is no-one funnier than C and she always has me in stitches with her humour. One cannot give that up. I believe that the few weeks you have to create should be completely trouble-free without emotional demands and ties. You create only a couple of times a year and those times must have absolute and undivided attention.

Thursday 4th July

Have my run, marvellous . . . sweat as I pound off twenty minutes of my life, the poisons oozing out of me, and feel a lot better . . . loads . . . now I can cope.

Come into the theatre to light and, of course, they are not ready, nor did they think to phone me. The canteen lady tells me off for not returning the used plates the other day . . . she was really upset last night . . . twice. Seeing me contrite she picks up several slabs of salami and bungs them on my plate for a treat, but I can't eat it.

Concentration going badly, lousy lights: a technician who can't understand what the play needs or what I communicate to him. The circus of translating like a beginner's guidebook. . . The stage manager who has to keep running out from behind a screen and the poor stand-ins who are actually employed to stand in for the actors. On top of this I feel love-sick, confused and after walking around, sitting in the park alone amongst the hundreds, I start to feel sick, lonely, desolate and need company, but as usual I am afraid to ask for it in case it craps up my work, in case the intensity of it all, the anticipation craps on what I am doing. I need to feel totally and utterly devoted to what I am doing. I want C to come and just have gentle walks and talks. You could go for broke and take risks, not be cowardly all your life, you might be pleasantly surprised but, as I said, you can't worship at two altars even if you are so lonely you can taste the blood in your mouth from a bleeding soul.

If the lighting were better we would achieve what we want, but not in the puny half-days they give us. You can't work after 3pm because they have to set up the next show and so you barely get going and you have to stop so that they can erect the set for the evening and so by this virtue they end up just lighting the actors and adding a bit of amber for atmosphere. Simplify more and more and have fewer cues. Easing up now! Just writing it out eases so much tension (too old for romance now and all that heart-thumping nonsense, but love is a terribly sweet, sickly thing).

Just one week to go, so hurl yourself into the play like a fiend and you have the stage all day Monday and Wednesday. No sweat! Only sweat is your life . . . there has to be life after the stage, there has to be.

Finish the first tiny piece and it looks good, though my heart aches, but as Günther says, "brick by brick". The atmosphere in the theatre is pure chaos — everybody shouting at once but it slowly comes like butter out of the churning milk. The opening with the citizens looks *fantastic* and so it begins well; it goes off but will keep shaping. It needs better light . . . Add cyclorama later, plus silhouette. Feeling dead but when it looks good feel better. Faster battle would be better.

Friday 5th July

Wake feeling utterly fucking miserable and it's largely my fault, although a great deal of it is due to the ghastly conditions at the theatre; it is beyond description — it's the fitting in with the other productions, since we can't start lighting until midday as it takes the staff two hours to strike the last set and put ours up and then this awful packing up by 3pm so that they can take ours down and put the other one up. So, four set changes in a day! So we inch forward a bit at a time in the three hours allotted us. At least Günther now sees that my scheme is working, although he seems to be betraying a rather arrogant superiority lately, watching me from behind my head to check up on things.

We run a few scenes and it improves. Some effects are beautiful and the scenes are starting to flow into each other. Günther is for the first time helpful as he watches. The dreary 'voices' scene, which I always thought would do as a kind of ordinariness in a sea of tumultuous excitement, he finds too naturalistic. I need that kind of direction to spur me on. I change the scene, with the citizens as oafs, silly, strutting idiots, and we put some spark back into the piece and the voices spring to life. But the *pièce de résistance* comes when Coriolanus makes his final pleading demands for their voices. I had this idea suddenly that they should respond as if he was a pop star, a great idol at a pop concert. It is a sensation. Just these words of direction give the piece the image that it lacked. They squirm and squeal with delight and Martin, the musician, plays a synthesized rock rhythm fitting with the delivery of the words. It demonstrably shows the awe the citizens have for Coriolanus and how easily led they are by a kind of group hysteria. It is a master stroke and is terribly funny. The burghers are now as cohesively linked as they were in the first scene when they march to demand corn. It is something that can happen at the end of rehearsal when one is looking at the clock and all but finished — demands slip away and you can go home satisfied and then in that moment of relaxation something may slip in like the big fish that tends to come just after the angler has dismantled his rod. It's a bonus, and now at last, after all these weeks, that scene is completed with a resounding crescendo in a way I never imagined. The last scene of all to go.

I go into the canteen and want merely a tea and the old dear behind the counter seems to have developed a mumsie crush on me and fills my plate with what I had always fancied but never had taken, since I can't eat during rehearsals. A plate of mashed potatoes, gravy, asparagus and some kind of fried bread with salami inside. I sit with Sona and the wets, whom I usually gravitate to, while the 'heavies' sit on the other table. Sona is a source of utter delight to me: her enthusiasm for all things beautiful, her love of form, painting, singing and movement.

We crawl into the rehearsal room and rehearse Aufidius meeting with Coriolanus the first time after exile. I don't think I have had to demonstrate so much to actors before but I also enjoy doing it but not to the extent that I have to delineate the details in each scene. We must show the two men's pleasure in each other's being, but not resort to those familiar bear-hugs so beloved in the theatre when two machos meet. We use an exercise where the two actors, holding each other by the wrists, keep balance while pulling each other's weight, much like a piece of sculpture of two wrestlers trying to pull each other over, but in this case the point is to retain equilibrium. It seems to please Rufus and the actor playing Aufidius, whom I am growing to like. I sense this earnest man's affection for me and I feel comfortable with him and he is physically very strong, as I discover when doing the exercise with him. He just needs more faith in himself but he is certainly a man without side and someone you could easily trust. So the greeting between the two men becomes a stylised gripping and holding and mock-wrestling. Rufus keeps worrying over tiny shrimps, but it works.

We again rehearse the scene where Volumnia and Virgilia come to beg Coriolanus for forgiveness and again it works well with Rufus as an impervious statue that is melted down by the tears of the wife and the persuasions of the mother working like a force in tandem. So while the mother utters the most persuasive polemic about loyalty and justice, his wife, with no words, creates the most powerful image of sexual, sensual and abiding love as she moves slowly round him, almost as an abject slave of his whim and at the same time an adoring and utterly loving woman. I imagine Rufus becomes distinctly troubled by this. Virgilia very slowly puts her long sensuous finger around his boots, rests her head against them, takes his hands, kisses the tips of his fingers and all this in perfect slow motion, not interfering with Lola's peroration. The scene is breathtaking. I gasp. I have never witnessed such adoring, passive love, and her face all the while stoic, statuesque, just etched with a long, deep sadness. At the end Coriolanus' will and body collapse. Volumnia's body has almost enveloped his as if an octopus was engulfing its prey. She rests the weight of her body against his — he collapses in tears. He can no longer move since he is trapped by women. I have to hold back my own tears — it is a sensation and comes from symbolising the rigid Coriolanus as a statue: impervious, cold, stiff.

Sona is pleased and as usual conveys it. Rufus senses he has broken down some barrier within himself and so when Coriolanus says to Aufidius that he couldn't help but be moved, we all believe it. We change the order of Aufidius' contempt speech to the end of the scene. Sona is happy in that we have taken a role that is usually small and meaningless in production and brought her into sharp focus with an idea that her remarkable body could breathe such life into.

During what is laughably called the lighting tech, my assistant, with her considerable integrity, misinterprets most cues. I feel like going home; I suffer far too much. Far in excess of what is necessary. This is beyond belief, the shouting backwards and forwards, the two assistants whose lack of experience further reinforces their own sullenness and they just sit and stare.

To break the ice I actually ask one after the session to have a coffee with me and as we walk along the familiar street she shows me a beautiful swimming pool that I had passed each day. (I had thought it was a railway station.) Going in, I see a huge area of grass, a pool, some tables to sit at under some blinds, a sunbathing area where they have set up ping-pong tables. I am astonished. What a delightful place: a marvellous escape, with an open-air café, just to relax, sit and watch. So I am pleased I had made some effort at conversation.

The assistant takes down all the moves and seems to quite like herself, very into the 'Do you like Robert Wilson?' school. Slim, studied in Paris, but hardly studied, she says, but 'lived' . . . and why not, indeed? She asks me what I do with myself here at night, this sounding like a line out of *Kvetch*. I try to appear normal and pretend that I haven't been going insane out of sheer desperation and cold-blooded horror. An aching, biting need to hold someone. I write my journal, I tell her, like one whose main concerns are academic with an obsessive quest to create, sometimes see my new German friend, the film producer, Rainer.

When I get home I slump in my bed in a semi-comatose state and try to nod off. No good, so I ring Rainer and he suggests that I join him and his friend in a typical Bavarian Biergarten. I am so overjoyed I nearly scream — or weep. I go downstairs and wait in the small bar, passing the time having a champagne and orange juice and watching the ridiculously obsessive tennis from Wimbledon. Their smug faces of grim satisfaction as they win a point or their sour pout if they don't makes me sick. Before I can hate them too much Rainer turns up and apologises for being late but he could not turn off his new computer, and I sympathise with the people who become slaves to their machines.

We drive to a beer garden on the verges of Munich, which is to a British beer garden what the Savoy is to a British prison. Here a couple of hundred happy burghers sit drinking beer from these copious tankards, steins, stoops, while munching giant twisted pretzels studded with salt. Bavarian food is served — huge wobbling slices of leberwurst or giant roast spare ribs. We queue for a couple of minutes and take a plate of ribs and one of sausages and sauerkraut. I hardly ever eat meat these days so the salted ribs taste phenomenal, really chewy, and dipped in a fabulous rich home-made sauce.

We sit and enjoy ourselves until Rainer's friend turns up. This man is head of two TV stations and so he probably doesn't need to talk and I don't care for these kind of self-important media bastards who control the mechanics of the arts while not making the arts themselves and yet adopt such an air of arrogant self-worth. I have never really felt comfortable with people who shine the seats of their arses behind desks and to whom you must beg for the time of day and arse-lick to have your work put on to film or video, when most of the bastards haven't a clue as to what you're about in the first place, especially some of the jerks I have had to deal with in London.

Rainer's friend sits sullenly and I am so exhausted and with so little spirit left in my charred and parched soul and yet still I try to squeeze out some communication. Rainer and I talk and he acts as some kind of TV host trying to entertain us by asking what was Eddie Murphy like to get on with and so for the fiftieth time I run through my ancient scripts, which I now know off by heart. After all, the film, *Beverly Hills Cop*, was released six years ago and I can still dine out on it! I had started out tonight full of optimism and now this man's presence depresses me with his industry babble of below-the-line and above-the-line waffle.

Then the friend's woman turns up — his current girlfriend. She is a round-faced pudgy idiot who keeps up an innocent grin the whole time, and then they stroke each other's arms under the table as if to say this is real and our meeting merely a prelude to amuse ourselves, so we don't have to give too much now since we have the carnality to enjoy later. Rainer and I act as some kind of entertainment centre — small, boring, irrelevant dead talk. I want to talk about pain, death, fear, love, passion, loss, struggle, but somehow couldn't get it out in that atmosphere. We roll a few movies about and Rainer is very charming and warm-hearted to me. At least I feel as if I have a friend in Munich.

Saturday 6th July

Suddenly a strange calm takes over me until I think of C before my madness starts again — only because I want it all to be perfect. Tried last night to 'cold turkey' and fell asleep eventually after four double scotches, two saki and one of the dispenser's small champagne bottles. I was in that sick phase but in the morning I run, feel better and only wish that rehearsals would take me away and keep me there. While I am rehearsing everything is fine.

We move the play onward, do some reasonable lighting. Rufus bristles with anger when preparing for the big fight scene with Aufidius since the cast joke and catcall as he takes his coat off. We have devised this 'street' ritual of slowly taking off your coat before you get stuck in to some fisticuffs. You normally take your coat off and your friend holds it. Rufus does this twice, once before the irate citizens and once with Aufidius. It's a threatening and dangerous-looking gesture implying a path of no return, since once you have made the ceremony of unrobing in front of everyone you can't very well change your mind! Today is the first day Rufus has the costume, a silvery long coat which looks ridiculous and which we will dye black. The cast giggle but Rufus is in no mood to be humiliated by levity. The 'voices' we discovered last week are still marvellous but much still needs to be done. No new ideas but all looks OK. We should have worked all day today but Rufus has a performance this evening.

I was feeling definitely wobbly about this whole business but now I'm on the plane trundling back once again for a weekend break in London and I feel OK. Just. I couldn't face returning to the hotel again, I just couldn't, but when I did return I discovered that work saved me. I started learning *Kvetch* and I began to relax as my mind was taken off its dog track and led through the woods into other terrains. It was boiling in my room and I took *Kvetch* and sat on the floor and learned some of the speeches. The energy that was being wasted, devoted and unleashed in worthless obsession was now diverted and I started to relax as the words and the thoughts of my play made a greater claim on me. So Arbeit does indeed Macht Frei! No question and *Kvetch* has a lot to get my teeth into and I start rehearsing it soon for the Edinburgh Festival, which I am delighted with.

I didn't want to leave the room and get the plane to London. I watched the clock tick tick past and missed plane after plane, but as the time of the last plane loomed up I weakened and found myself in trouble once again. Calmly I packed and took a cab. I didn't want to do this but my feet were leading me there. I wanted to see Rufus work and watch his young vital energy engage us both. I wanted to walk to the theatre where I belonged and go to see C in the countryside tomorrow in Hof. Instead, like a junkie, I followed my needful obsession. I may feel like a junkie but I did say I would return to London this week-end. I even faxed my desire to go back. I take the junkie route. However, finish off what you began. I wouldn't have been able to get back from Hof before 11am anyway. And the way this company functions they would all get into hysterics and start running to Günther if I turned up late again.

I know I should never have started this crap but now I'm on the plane my spirit is very relaxed and calm so it can't be as bad as my head thought it might be. When we took off I saw the glorious sun-baked green countryside and I regretted that I wouldn't walk in the woods with C this weekend but please God I will do it next week! Please all of you forgive me!

I had been invited to the theatre tonight to see Schiller's *The Robbers*, which Rufus is in, but I would have sat in the theatre watching an incomprehensible play and sweated out my angst. You might have sat through two hours of turgid rubbish and been kicking yourself. No matter, follow it through. Last night was murder, couldn't sleep. I suffered the torments of the damned. Try and rehearse *The Tell-tale Heart* this Sunday? OK, go to Brighton. At least you can do all those things today. In fact you could return Sunday night! Enough! Enough! No time. You did what you had to do — but did you *have* to? Aye, there's the rub. Still, not so sweaty on it and maybe it's OK. I'm losing weight. I look over Clara's Germany and *wish I hadn't done it!*

The play slowly grows and gets together on stage. The fight with the Tribunes should be better, and it needs a special light. The punch-up works well and Menenius still fails to remember a single move. However, 'it goes', as they say. (Why didn't I dissolve the whole thing, I started to dissolve it but then I do get roused when I think of her.) I am starting to enjoy watching the play and but for their stupid system and bungling lights we would be ahead of the game.

I felt good this morning and sweaty from the run around King Ludwig. I didn't want it to end. I wanted someone to chain me to a post like Ulysses so that I couldn't leave. I wanted to be chained and whipped to prevent me getting on this plane. I sought the comfort of *work*. Studying my lines took my mind away from this fever. I calmed down. Stopped sweating and my pulse rate decreased. Sona called and I wished I could have seen her and had dinner after the show. What memories I might have had and inner strength and adventures in the country. How my life might have changed. I am beginning to get used to Munich and am even developing an affection for these actors in spite of all and am no longer reluctant to come back to Germany.

Günther sat next to me at rehearsal today with his assistant by his side. His assistant picked his nose furiously and I do believe feasted on the delicatessen he found there. Does this childish habit suggest infantilism of the anal retentive — scooping out shavings of dried sputum and then returning same to mouth? Very off habit. If I were ever tempted to explore those caverns Clara would pull me up with a sharp "Send me a postcard when you get there". . . very repulsive and make a mental note not to shake the assistant's hand ever again.

Birgitta and Gisela invited me to dinner tomorrow night and so I've blown that too. Birgitta was terribly nice yesterday and we had a sushi together and she told me a fascinating story about a Jewish director who was in love with her. (I am only really interested these days in people's love lives.)

I now understand Kafka so well. When he was to meet his beloved in Berlin he didn't stop kvetching, cancelling and then going. For the highly sensitive mind love acts like a rottweiler that has been set loose in your system and you can barely control it. Writing the pure distillations of his soul poor Kafka was unable to fulfil them in the flesh. In fact, mortified, poor man, and writing, writing, writing. I now like Munich and will offer my services to keep the play 'well tuned'. I like the little places and the See café, my Italian café round the corner, the Kafer deli, the park, the English Garden, Leopoldstrasse, my lovely hotel, Dieter Opitz, of course, and now my familiarity with the cast.

Sunday 7th July

Big lesson of my life. . . took myself to hell and back and for why? I sit in the idyllic warmth of this beautiful outdoor café and fling myself like a dumb golem in the direction of my obsession. I waited at the airport and actually tried to miss the plane but I found my feet irrevocably moving beneath my body. And what did I gain? A further descent into the maelstrom of fear. Gutless to refuse to go and gutless to stay. I could have stayed and showed the wonders of the world. When you risk you gain tenfold and of course nothing worth having is without a certain element of risk.

Tonight we light Act Two. Although there are two TV sets offstage to guide Ronda, our very charming ex-dancer stage manager, the ineptness of the organisation still reminds me of the Chingford Amateur Operatic Society. This beautiful theatre, with its gilded balcony and rococo style ceiling, is defaced by a lighting rig that tears into its face like a steel trap into an animal. Wagner must be turning in his grave in Valhalla. The lighting man hasn't a clue what is going on and when we have a cue he looks in the text book to see where it comes, when most of the cues are on actions. He keeps cawing, "I haven't seen it . . . I haven't seen it", which is a disgrace for a lighting rigger, particularly in this case when we must translate a director's wishes into German.

Monday 8th July

Of course, I could have stayed and travelled back this morning. What's a half an hour late? I come in and of course they're not nearly ready . . . could have done this, could have done that. It's OK, but next time take your balls in your hand. C will come and I will show her everything, including the canteen. I seem to want to show those small and yet to me intimate details of my life, like where I sit every day in my break: the workers' canteen, which is such a German institution. Had a run this morning and sweated away freely, which I love. I am glad to be back in Munich. Hell and back . . . as I ran through the trees I thought, how beautiful, we could have run together through the trees. Not been stuck in that little hole. There is life outside the stage — there is!

What you sow, you reap — Munich might have sealed it, but you made your work your God, which is right for the time. She said sweet things like, "If I was with you I wouldn't allow you to worry", and I believed it. Change gear — the play's the thing.

We work well today — start strong and continue. It looks great, though Günther has nothing to say about the most sensational death scene ever that Rufus does. Having been impaled he shakes like a horrifying insect in its death throes . . . a pierced cockroach . . . his long thin limbs twitching as an insect refusing to die. Aufidius then puts his sword through him and impales him to the floor. He twists around the sword but can't leave the floor to which he is impaled. What a movie this would make!

I work the scene again with Coriolanus and the Tribunes and try to restore its balletic qualities, the sudden freezes when they see each other, the feints, the rush across, the resistance by Coriolanus' two allies who attempt to defuse the situation, palms outward to the chest of Coriolanus while looking anxiously at the Tribunes, trying to allay the row from exploding. Menenius cannot recall a move and so this kind of staging is becoming difficult and as usual he looks to the stage manager for help each time and so kills the flow of the scene. However, he has a magnificent instrument in his vocal cords. The scene works well enough.

Sometimes Rufus lacks the variation in tone and sounds

too adenoidal. He takes Coriolanus very seriously but needs a bit of street 'shtick' . . . . The scene explodes when the citizens race on like *West Side Story* or a flock of locusts descending on a wheat field.

Since Giorgi, our replacement Tribune, is out ill our 'assistant' reads in to give the others the cues and moves. Now a funny thing occurs to me on the way to the forum. When as an assistant she speaks perfect English, writes down all the moves and is highly educated, Paris, Sorbonne etc. . . . . "lived rather than studied", I can suddenly see her and thousands like her. Well-educated, cultured, favourite movie directors are Lina Wertmuller, Fassbinder, Herzog etc., and never watches rubbish American shit, thank God. But as she is an academic and not an actress her skills mean absolutely nothing as she reads the lines looking wimpish and weak on the stage; suddenly in my mind's bilious eye she seems listless, pathetic, dull. Of course she's not trained to project her voice but there is something in her standing on stage that shows her in an unfair light, and that she uses her brains to manipulate the knowledge of academia.

The big raging voices of the actors are the sounds of the people. Their guts, fury and desire to give, to create, to risk and tear their voices out of their stomachs, to bare themselves and to sacrifice not only their minds but their egos, the physical live person. To risk humiliation. To sweat in fear before going out there. To expose and try to reveal the heart of the dead writer and unite it with a living heart that it may give life. The actors put themselves at the service of humanity. To live and to amuse, to move and excite, and he or she is still treated like a scourge and a joke at times, a person of no thoughts but a writer's appendage. Well, on the stage at the moment I see the lacklustre hue of the intellectuals who fart with their mouths at conferences and in coffee houses and who have

- 141 -

opinions on everything except themselves, since sleeves are never held up for scrutiny. I wish with all my heart to make humanity laugh and cry and squeeze myself into a knot of pain in order to do it and I am glad and expect no thanks since it is a privilege to be doing this. Looking at this slightly trendy lady on stage with her ever-so-superior attitude and fitted designer jeans, lisping out the words with no energy, I see the actors as lawless, simple and good-natured workers who train their voices to give and to boom out. Rich, big voices, designed to express and project and I realise that what acting is is giving. Acting is a great leveller, like boxing. Your class, money, family are worthless on a stage: on a stage it is who and what *you* are.

The actors now feel themselves to be part of the team and since we rid ourselves of the renegade wimp who tried to destroy our teamwork we have closed up the nasty abscess his presence caused. Of course, one of the actors today is sick and comes on wearing his neck in a truss. (He had actually been in a car bang-up and suffered whiplash.) I can't bear it and I declare that never have I seen or come across such physical vulnerability in my life and that it fitted in with their constant whining. The whining threw their minds or bodies off centre and made them in fact accident prone and although I was guilty of a little exaggeration I felt the main tenor of my argument was sound. I have always found that it is the whingers who become ill. This is borne out of twenty years of directing. Of course, the whingers generally blame you for their own shortcomings and seek attention for the difficulties you impose. They will seek security in their old non-committed style of acting. The accidents are somehow part of the syndrome but of course not always; that would be most unfair to any great actor who has had time off for injuries sustained in very much greater exertions.

Decisions must be made. Come home after wonderful pasta

in my favourite bar, with a beautiful Beaujolais. Seeing a fax in my hole in reception I grab it with mental satisfaction but am disturbed by its seeming brevity. I don't even read it in the lift but, like a cat, keep my little mouse of joy to savour in my room. I get in and unfold it to discover it isn't from the person I wish above all to hear from. I am so disappointed I screw the paper into a ball. No, this is not what I wanted. The devil adores trapping the brain. Then I fall into an immediate sleep. Fortunately I am nearly finished with this show and so I will have time to let other things into my life. My sleep which was so sweet turns into nightmares again. I have more decisions to make, whether I do this or that when I return, and my brain chews into them trying to tear them into little bits. I have *The Tell-tale Heart* to rehearse and record next week. I must work as soon as I get back or do I say yes, yes and yes? That's what I'd like to do but don't quite have the bottle. De-escalate and stick to your work.

Tuesday 9th July

I get to the theatre at 11.05am when I made a call to start at 11am. The actors were called to get into costumes at 10am. I don't need to see them get ready like Mum watching the babies getting dressed at kindergarten, since I prefer to see costumes in action on the stage. Rita, one of our stage managers, had rung the hotel saying everyone's waiting for you. I said "Who's everyone?" like the cleaner and the cooks? I said I made a call for an 11am start and once again my sloppy assistant with the long morbid face and the other one I can now barely look at have fucked up yet again. I tear in, saying we had this conversation last last night . . . I had been in the theatre from 11am to 10pm the day before! I said the first hour for the actors' costumes and lights to set up. "No," the Dummkopf says, "You said 10am." I blow off the top of Vesuvius . . . she has made me look as if I was irresponsibly cruising in at any time. I feel sick even looking at these two waxen, smug, self-satisfied German faces who have really been of so little help in the past five weeks. An appalling lack of theatre fundamentals but were just there somehow to learn off me without giving too much back except their constant bungling. Perdita Kark, my stage manager in England, is now looking to me like a guardian angel.

Then we start. The costumes are unbelievably bad and that is the highest compliment. I despise yet another amateur whom Günther saw fit to give to me. I had even shown her the New York costumes designed with some flair by Martin Pakledinaz. I wished to actually improve on his designs, worthwhile as they were, but these are monstrous. We discuss the citizens' torn jackets, sleeves ripped off, rough Italian peasants, knee-length boots, leather of course, black shirts, crumpled trilby. Then they whip off their jackets and lo and behold underneath they are the soldiers of Coriolanus with leather belts and straps over the shoulder. Bang, they add sunglasses (perfect mask) and they are the gang of Aufidius. The designer couldn't even bring herself to get the black leather boots, which does and says all, so designed a kind of sock with a small cross on one side (the Romans); turn the sock down and *voilà*, there is some kind of symbol of the Volscians! They look like Bavarian mountain climbers and not only could you not read or understand this simple code meant to tell the audience that they are different, it couldn't even be seen past the second row. Such meaningless trivia with the socks all at different lengths. The poor girl is another amateur who had only been an assistant before now and proved her amateur status by arguing that her petty designs were good. Whereas it is the director's job to say if it works or not and even if they were works of genius the director has to approve the total effect and in this case it isn't a taste clash, they are just fucking dismal, and even Günther for once comes down on my side. But it wasn't even the design. It was the fulsome smug intolerance to me and the bloated, "I think they're good" that I couldn't stand.

Then Coriolanus comes on in what looks like a silver housecoat you slip on in the morning to make breakfast, with crosses on it like it had been stamped in a toaster. That I had asked for him to be in black leather like a raven, a big billowy coat, but black didn't seem to have occurred to the —. So the silver dissolves into the back-cloth, which is a silvery grey sky. This is a wicked waste of my time and everyone else's. "Where's the black coat I asked for?" "I sprayed it down," she whispers limply, from her designer-haircut head.

But the *coup de grâce* was Aufidius, who looked like a messenger, not a motor-bike messenger, but one who rides a moped. The designer had simply bought a cheap leather jacket like something you might get in C & A and put grey streaks on it. Then she had bought khaki trousers with those bulging pockets at the side that you put maps in and look so stupid as to defy description, and *brown boots!* We had talked of surrealism, a kind of 'Mad Max' head to toe in leather and metal, a rebel, an anarchist, dangerous. But this was back in amateur concepts, no energy and the distillations of the bourgeois class. I recognised the same lack of drive, conviction and academia and fart-wind coming out of their mouths . . . we had talked for ages and ages, and this is like we never talked. For the costume of poor Aufidius I reserve my greatest spleen since not only was the actor still no fucking good but he was growing and this made him look like a prize arsehole! I had shown the wretch the amazing costumes that our black Aufidius had worn in New York: a one-piece suit in silver, a hat in chain mail, sawn-off gloves.

I say to the designer this is truly wrong, it's actually ghastly, to which she replies: "I think it's very good." I say please don't give me your opinion since we're not having a discussion after the show, like critics. It's my business to direct it and cohere the elements — I can't stand arguing whether it's good or bad. The costume is pathetically real, with little zips all over the place that she thought gave it some taste of style.

The women's costumes simply defy description and I won't even go into it but think of what that lady who sells Avon make-up might wear at night, that lady who comes to your door with her samples. Volumnia looks like a shapeless sack and a scarlet wig pulled down over her face gives her the curious profile of the Elephant Man. However, our little art school designer thought it was wonderful. I think of Silvia Jansen, my designer on *Usher*, hacking it across the world with her one kid and no father and turning out great inventions from her wild and bizarre imagination and how she would have relished the job.

We run the act once and it looks dire. But the second time, as the actors rip up their clothes a bit and get used to the boots (we're getting rid of the sox) it starts to really take off. Suddenly it looks powerful and the chorus are sure of the moves since they are the pulse and the heart of the play, giving it its momentum while the principals allegedly give it the brains. I now give my first note session. I am complimentary to a fault and say they need have no fear since there were truly fine and exciting moments in the play culminating in an extraordinary final scene when the words and moves seem frozen in space. I was very excited by the way they had rallied round the theme and now they had reactions from their other colleagues who had sneaked into the theatre during rehearsal so they were getting some very positive feedback. Some of the play had the atmosphere of Goya's paintings and sometimes it was like Chirico.

I go out feeling somewhat better and have an interview with a critic! We go to the public swimming pool with its tables and lawns that I had discovered a few days ago with one of my assistants. The critic reminded me of Lotte Lenya, with her long, horse-like face, but she had a laborious style of speaking like she had sat in coffee shops all her life and at dinner tables, discussing endlessly the Kammerspiel's latest production of *The Robbers*. Her face is full of opinions of the sweat and toil of others. She then asks in her dreary, laboured and heavy style what I have done! "Don't you have a press kit?" I ask. No, they didn't give her one. So she sits and needs to write in longhand — "Please speak slowly" — what have I done? Well, I have just finished one of the most exciting runs of a play that I have ever seen in my life, just an hour ago, and to be dragged down by this horsey, slow pedant was not my idea of a tea-break.

I had just had a chat with Sona beside the pool before the critic met me at the theatre and we walked back. With Sona our conversation raced so that we took off in mutual flights of excitement, keeping each other airborne by the energy and precious air of each other's love and purpose. With some people conversation does that and the molecules collide into each other and thoughts are generated that you normally would never encounter and so I hauled myself up the ladder of her thought and she did mine.

With this decayed Munich critic who orders a large brandy as soon as we arrive and already seems half cut, I feel I am crawling along on my belly. Along broken glass in fact. Every step is painful as she takes it all down in her labour-saving longhand. "Why did you want to do *Coriolanus?*" she burps. "I didn't," I say, "it meant nothing to me, a play is a means to express your purpose in the art of theatre and the act of uniting a team of actors, musicians and designers to tap the essence of the play according to the time we live in."

I remember Joe Papp ringing me in Dublin asking me if I was interested in directing *Coriolanus* at the Public. He had just read a review in the *New York Times* of my Irish production of *Salome* and in the typical way they work in the USA they strike as it occurs to them. While the iron is hot, so to speak. It was the first concrete offer I had from him. I accepted it in a good mood and liked the title of the play but had only read it once years ago and seen it once in a production at the National that I could make no sense of whatsoever. A few weeks before starting the show I wanted to cancel; I was overcome by a bout of fear. As I was performing *Greek* at the Wyndhams *Coriolanus* kept jumping into my head. I was afraid . . . a New York opening of a play I had never worked out in the secret confines of my own actors. I had no idea. I read and re-read the play, falling asleep at some sections. I tried to concentrate on it but one forgets that the seeing is in the doing, and not in the reading. Trust old intuition. I tried to recall old productions. Not many images remained of a recent production with the redoubtable and fiery McKellen, except some confetti coming down from the flies as he comes into Rome! I looked at the Olivier photos of his Coriolanus as if trying to find a clue that would kick-start me off. In the end my own first image gave me the play, the force exploding out of the frustration and hunger of the people and their eruption onto the stage. That helped me fill in the rest once I had put down the king post.

I can't begin to explain this to the critic, who keeps saying, "Sorry, could you repeat that? . . ." I start to feel my head growing heavy and nodding. Her voice and plodding manner are making me sick as she sits there knowing nothing and smoking with her cigarette-holder clamped in her teeth. Slowly, slowly writing . . . "Sorry, sorry, sorry, could you repeat it slowly?" I close my eyes in pain and she takes the hint and shoots off. Poisoned against me now and ready to fire off a bad review, which in due course, true to her lousy form, she does. A snake if ever I saw one.

In the evening I try to walk off my angst with a long trek to the English Garden and be a Bavarian and eat a sausage and sauerkraut with one of those huge beers. The weather is overcast and warm. I walk swiftly, sweating profusely and buy a huge red sausage and a half of Weissbier. The sausage tastes almost too rich in meat after the English junk. It is red and raw with crisp charcoaled skin. As I stick my fork in it spits all over my shirt like it was alive. I am stuffed full halfway through and then the rains come and I leave my beer and scoot home. It pours. I run, zigzagging through the garden, trying to shelter from time to time under the branches of the big trees. I get home and lie on my bed. I unpeel and let the sound of the rain send me to sleep.

Wednesday 10th July

I wake up deaf in both ears. I can hardly hear a thing and the orange sticks are serving only to increase my deafness. I feel wretched, empty and isolated, as if this was a further punishment in my sense of withdrawing from the world. I feel like crying. I can't hear the play and feel remote from the world. I think that stress has poured its sweaty angst into my body, congealing itself into wax, and deafened me. I complain of my woe to Dieter, who straight away rings round for a doctor who could see me immediately, and we jump in a cab and go to her clinic. The doctor is an extremely attractive woman, in her early thirties I should imagine, and is an ear, nose and throat specialist. She treats me like I was made of velvet and rolls up and down on her wheeled chair pouring various unguents into me. She has bare brown legs under her starched white uniform and is mightily pretty. She treats me in the space of a few minutes and suddenly the world comes hissing back to life again. I return to the stage like a born-again man with new ears. I am very much struck by the young doctor and think of her studying for years to be so skilled as to have her own practice. (She did eventually see the show and actually wrote to me complimenting me on the production. I wrote back but never heard from her again.)

They're frank here but stupidly maladroit. One of the actors, a young Turk, and so easily familiar with his directors in the post-Hitler age of anal indolence, said to me after all the angst and suffering I had gone through to make the best possible show of my life: "We wondered if you were just coming here for the money. . ." I suppose he realises that German theatres pay two to three times what the mean Brits pay. Then Wolfgang, whom I had credited with a modicum of intelligence, says: "Couldn't we just as easily do this play with people off the street?" I suppose he is right. I could just as easily do the choreography for the play with skilled kids off the street but then the acting couldn't be done like that since it needs determined skills and the stuff that he says could be done by amateurs is group work, ensemble and team work and needs group co-ordination and these are the areas where the actors would be in the dressing rooms or standing around with their dicks in their hands bored to death or getting pissed in the theatre bar as I saw in the UK. What else could they do with themselves? Here at least they were functioning and kept alive in the spirit of the play and in fact what they did, although working as a group, would not be so effective without the skills of an actor.

The actor I had to sack goes to the press in the spirit of a Nazi informer. He lies to the yellow press of Munich, who don't even bother to contact me for my version but are content to print the scumbag's lies. He says I didn't discuss the character as if the character wasn't already in the play of Shakespeare but like many of these pap-fed, spoon-fed whiners wants your attention to what is obvious. Not only did we discuss the part, we showed, demonstrated the very body language of the characters which the other actors leapt upon. But people who don't work intuitively and who spend hours discussing the obvious as a form of artistic evasion always complain, since their internal rhythms are so dead.

Another actor asks questions in a perpetual whine and when things momentarily break down there is a collective whining. The paradox is that they are really doing quite well and some are very good in the roles. There are scenes of considerable excitement and verve so it is not all who complain, but I sense that they feel obliged to, since this is probably the first time in the history of the theatre when a production has been brought in within five weeks and in such good nick!

The music is one second late for Rufus and so he pulls a long face, scowls, whines and looks ready to break down, when so much of the play is working beautifully this morning . . . But at the same time I understand the frustration of his character, which is coming to life and is still in the raw naked stage of development.

Of course the props, few as they are, are missing. The stage management didn't request them and the technical crew look to each other as the culprits for the omission.

Today Aufidius starts to appear more imposing in his now all-leather outfit and has lost the motorbike, or rather moped, messenger look.

Tonight we have the first entire run-through of the play and the stage floor is now looking better and is mostly black, with the four grey squares in the centre. Günther is shouting at the designer for not dealing with the costumes and props, thus taking over from my spleen, and she is unlikely to say to *him*, "Well, *I* think it looks good . . ."

Thursday 11th July: D-day

Apart from constant background 'noises', which were the demons in my mind, the day goes well. Get in early after a horrendous night of angst. I was thinking of the bare-legged doctor in her gleaming surgery, surrounded by her instruments and her cleverness. The whole theatre seems to know about my ears.

We run the first act, which lasts one hour 45 minutes. It looks well and starts strongly. Rufus makes a good slow entrance as if in a Western. The two senators now have good costumes and the designer has at least created good lines in the long coats they wear and which swing back as they walk. The coat Rufus wears is now dyed black, the colour I wanted from the beginning, and no longer looks like a nightie. Rufus tries a hairpiece, which gives the leonine effect of a mane tumbling down his back. Why not try anything at this stage and see? Günther comes running up saying, "Was it your idea, the hair? It looks silly." He now behaves like many producers who once they see the first run-through are convinced that it is the only way to do it and resist strongly any change lest you spoil the first impression. I actually think the wig gives Rufus a vulpine animal quality and certainly is not so vast a change as to warrant such an outburst.

Menenius, after his first real promise, appears to have got stuck and from time to time seems bewildered and is forgetting his lines and still looks to the stage management corner for his three or four simple moves. Bernhard Baier as Sicinius, on the other hand, relishes the work and continually invents. The style suits him and gives him a framework in which to grow and which it is intended to, so it gives me much pleasure to watch him, never complaining and always inventing or telling me stories about his theatre in East Germany and the parts he played.

Coriolanus' exit in the first scene with the senators is now completely and utterly chilling as he goose-steps off, which Rufus does with great physical power. He thrusts those long legs in the air, his cockscomb fluttering with the vibration and his coat swirling behind him. It makes the hairs on the neck rise. The two senators also reproduce the walk. In Rufus I see now such a hunger for the role and he also continually invents and explores the character. He now seems confident in each of his monologues and handles them with great control. He grows stronger and is less out of breath. Unlike Chris Walken, Rufus takes part in the battle scenes and is like the raging centre of a whirlpool. He does not watch at a distance but thrives in its inferno. He performs the fighting motions like some terrible black satanic creature pouncing and tearing at his prey, his winged coat flying about him like an eagle.

Lola is getting better and Christiane, who had such trouble with her butterfly speech, is now very good. The movement of horses and battle has never been so sharp and improves on the New York version and now that Aufidius' costume has become more menacing and 'dangerous' his own performance grows in confidence. The chorus now have the boots I requested originally, though much time, money and labour was spent on the insane design of the silly sox which have now been discarded. The act works well and we spend only three hours on it and have a break until 6pm when we run the whole. No props or set problems and no all-nighters to deal with the excrescences of a director's whims. Just three hours and the act is smooth as butter.

In the break I walk into the Munich sunshine and sit in the Kafer café and eat my arugula and Parmesan. I return to the theatre at 5.30 and have a tea. The old lady behind the bar now treats me regularly and bungs me a doughy cake which has some icing powder on it.

At 6pm we start and I am full of joyous anticipation. I actually love looking at what I have created and when it works and the machine is tightened up and ready to fly I feel no less exaltation than did the Wright Brothers on the first flight. The play takes on another element when it starts to run and a kind of magical spirit enters into it. A group emotion winds itself around the play and infuses it with a beating heart. The cyclorama comes up and its pale blue sheen imparts a beautiful sense of space . . . sometimes it has the look of a medieval painting. The sky varies from an angry red to a clear, restful infinite blue.

I ask for a beer for the first time in the theatre and decide to enjoy it. Günther comes in and out, whispering little suggestions in my ear, nudging me on the shoulder. Then he goes out for a while, then he comes back, then goes out, and does this several more times until his very presence is anathema. I know he wishes to show his interest and concern but it is spoiling my joy and therefore my perception in the examination of the run.

The first act goes well and we have a break and so I look for Rufus so that I might communicate my enthusiasm for the clarity of the performance, but I can't even find his dressing room. When I do see him I have to claw my way through the talk. In fact I always have to gain his attention by saying "Rufus" two or three times since he seems always to be engaged in his mighty concerns, and this galls me somewhat since his performance was a collaborative act and some say he has never been better. Of course, there is a certain amount of possessiveness and jealousy on my part like a Mum who can't bear to see her fledgeling leave the nest. He is now Coriolanus and sometimes with a vengeance and in his new confidence he pulls himself out of my orbit and makes his own trajectories. I watch it happen and still have the desire to see him accountable to me and to seek my eyes for approval, but he must go his own way and, like the older parent, one only hopes for visits and acknowledgement. Of course, no-one expresses any joy from the act which has gone so well, or appreciation.

Act Two, and it works even better! The usually dull 'voices' scene is better than ever since we discovered the rock concert approach and now Rufus really socks it to them. The last scene is worth waiting for as it deliberately but slowly increases temperature as Aufidius warns his surly crew about the dangers of giving in to Coriolanus. They sit in a macabre line, still and listening like crows on an electric cable. Black, satanic and merciless. Coriolanus enters full of optimism and hope with his peace 'proposal' held in the case by one of the senators. We have already discussed the scene and it is played quietly and effectively, building moment by moment to its ultimate crescendo. Rufus' jacket is already soaking wet and shows the stain down his back since the designer didn't think of making two suits or creating a change after the interval. The two protagonists argue, circle and Coriolanus is stabbed by the entire group like a pincushion. They pull out their swords but he refuses to die and is therefore pinned to the ground by the merciful sword of Aufidius.

Still he refuses to die and twists on the sword as we rehearsed and one can almost feel what that must be doing to his internal organs. But he refuses to die. Eventually, not to be killed like a beast, he pulls the sword out of his stomach and holds it aloft before expiring. A notable and terrifying death. (What a film this would make.)

The first run-through is over and it has gone well. I have no notes. I hate notes. I would rather rehearse scenes that don't work than sit with a whole gaggle of people in front of me. I go to Günther for some response. It has truly gone well and I am satisfied if not quite excited. The new inventions and the daring into life of new scenes has paid off. The first run-through is over and there is an air of excitement after all the chat, arguments, phone calls back and forth from Munich to Joanna Marston, my London agent, the whining cast, the fears, the accusations, the doubts, the lack of faith. At last now we see rising out of all this something special and even beautiful. All two and three-quarter hours of it. So I go to Günther for a tiny bit of praise after all the lonely nights and the torture and the suffering and the missing and the angst I had left behind in the UK. The misery. The never-to-be-had drinks or dinner with my comrades except for the darling Sona. The endless meals alone which I also enjoyed and enjoyed creating the tapestry of words that would carry this story forward to the end of time but wanted a warm word of praise from him. The boss. The Intendant. The father figure. His teutonic soul can barely utter a sound. "Yes, it's coming together," he says . . . "Don't you think Lola is too loud?" I am facing him. "I'll tell her," I say. "Perhaps she should be more polemic," I add.

I rush into the street to get out of that place. Wolfgang ("You could use people from the street") is outside. It looks good, I tell him, and you could be proud of your achievement. The cast are astonished to be allowed home, since usually they sit for two hours having 'notes'. Fortunately I do my homework in rehearsal and rehearse so thoroughly that they don't need to sit for two hours trying to unravel the director's ineptitude. Notes congeal the atmosphere and you can't give an actor acting notes in front of his colleagues. So I call a rehearsal so that we can rehearse any small deficiencies. Wolfgang says he now enjoys it and refutes his earlier statement. He is about to ride away on his Yamaha 500. He's wearing shorts, bare legs exposed to the elements, and that's dangerous if you come off a bike. I warn him to cover up when riding a motorbike but young people never learn until they come off. They want to be tough. I was like that. I rode a Gold Wing on the freeways of LA, wearing only a cloth cap to keep my brains in if I came off.

Tomorrow is the second preview and on Saturday the press come. As far as *I'm* concerned it's over. My task is done. Sona and I share a pasta.

Friday 12th July

It is hot as hell and C arrives at the station where I meet her and introduce her to Munich. Her train is unusually a few minutes late, which is odd for Germany where the health of the country's pulse is measured by the punctuality of the trains — like, get that right and everything else will fall into place, but just as I am deliberating on this the platform's digital display board answers my thoughts by announcing that the train will be approximately five minutes late. Good! Time to scoff a pair of frankfurters, which somehow taste even better on station platforms.

C arrives in a blaze of sunshine and smiles and we jump into a cab and I am strangely excited in showing her my new city and we head directly for the Kafer deli where we unburden ourselves of our stories. I have the arugula while she eats some sea creature that looks as if it had wandered into rotary blades.

Bruce Payne, who played Eddie in my last version of *Greek*, sends me a best wishes fax from LA, which also points out that he used to pass Hitler's old residence at 16 Prince Regent Strasse, which I also had unknowingly passed each day on my way to the park. The large brooding house looks unused and sits away back from the street and, with its iron-grilled windows and canopy of dark green ivy, the heavy gates well locked, has a satanic air about it. I stood by it and studied it for some time as if my senses could still detect his evil spirit.

The second preview tonight is a good show and I enjoy it all the more for being able to share it with someone and having another pair of eyes doubles my enjoyment of it. We watch the show with the stage management from the special box at the back of the theatre where I imagine Hitler would undoubtedly have sat for his Wagnerian evenings, but the theatre chief, Herr Everding, now always sits here on first nights.

Saturday 13th July

The press night arrives and C and I take a slow stroll down to the theatre and the long street now becomes charted with memories since I am well aware that this is the last time I will see it. The pharmacy where I got my detonator pills, the Kafer deli, which gave me so many peaceful hours and wide-eyed strolls around their cornucopia of delights, past the swimming pool, which for a month I thought was the entrance to the station, past the old houses and small dull shops, past the exterior of the theatre with its display of photographs showing what was currently on and in whose stiff images I would try and analyse the characters of the actors, and then up the sweeping staircase to the theatre.

The sun is shining down brightly which clashes with the nature of the play, which is dark and violent, and so everybody is taking the sunshine and eating ice creams in their smart evening finery. The foyers are filling up with the cultural and financial elite of Munich and the neat little sandwiches are in evidence on the counters which so impressed me when I first arrived, which seems so long ago.

We take our seats and wait expectantly. The drum explodes into life and the actors erupt on to the stage and the play progresses smoothly from there. C likes it more, as I do now we are nearer the heat of the action.

The interval: we go outside but I don't want to mix self-consciously with the audience so I take C to see the canteen which has been my home for the duration. I like the canteen. It reminds me of a kibbutz canteen in Israel where you feel protected in the egalitarian atmosphere of common goals. The actors are sitting in there and I tell them it is going well.

The second act works even better and the lights go down. Spontaneous explosion of applause and even bravos, though less than there were for the previews now with so many dignitaries and critics in.

Of course, as is normal in Europe, I am summoned on to the stage to take my bow with the actors. The applause swells and then I hear distinctly 'BOOS ! . . .' Is there some claque out there? Perhaps allies of the sacked actor who has rallied support against me? I think it could be, since they seem to be coming from just one area. I counteract the indignity by smiling and yet the boos make me feel outraged for the work I have done. I raise my hand as if the boos were roses which I was gratefully gathering. My raised hand now unconsciously clenches into a fist as a reaction to the scorn of the booers and the actors reassure me that anything that goes against the norm is booed in Munich.

We all celebrate at a little party afterwards in the other theatre's canteen, a much larger theatre which is being restored. We are all very happy and shake hands and say farewell and C and I walk out into the warm, balmy air.